The Autobiography of Herbert E. Grings
His Testimony and Missionary Service in the Belgian Congo

By
Herbert Ernest Grings

Revisions by Louise Grings Champlin
and Matthew Champlin

Text Copyright © 2012 Matthew C. Champlin
All Rights Reserved

Cover design by Sarah Roberts, www.reflectingthedesigner.com

Pictures used by permission of Grings family members.

Originally printed by Living Spring Printing Press in 1963.

Table of Contents

FOREWORD 4

PREPARATION FOR MISSIONARY SERVICE 5

EARLY MISSIONARY SERVICE IN CONGO 15

MINISTRY YEARS IN THE USA 34

FAMILY MINISTRY IN CONGO AGAIN 53

TRANSITIONS AND VARIOUS TRAVELS 70

EPILOGUE 87

APPENDIX: HERBERT AND RUTH'S CHILDREN 91

FOREWORD

Over the years, numerous and repeated requests have been made for a reprint of *The Autobiography of Herbert E. Grings*. The original book was printed in Hong Kong in 1963 with only four thousand copies. They went worldwide, and the supply was quickly diminished. Recently, Mrs. Jan Van Hee published *No Turning Back,* an adaptation of the *Autobiography* specifically for a younger generation. It has received a warm and wide welcome, but it doesn't replace the original *Autobiography* written in the first person. Therefore, we are now attempting to respond to those who have requested this release and apologize for the long delay in meeting the desire of so many dear friends and long-time supporters.

Louise Grings Champlin, the last remaining of the five Grings children, has made a few corrections and added this Foreword, an Epilogue concerning the rest of Herbert Grings' life, and an Appendix concerning the five Grings children. Some additional research and new formatting from great-grandson Matthew Champlin will enhance the account. Sarah Grings, a great-granddaughter, has also assisted.

We now release the book to you, many of whom have helped by prayer and encouragement over the years. Our earnest prayer is that this book will again be used of God in encouraging its readers to greater commitment and confidence in the God whom Herbert Grings willingly and fervently followed to the uttermost parts. Herbert proved unfailingly the faithfulness of God, and we who have walked in his footsteps and maintained that heritage desire only that Christ be lifted up and all men be drawn to Him (John 12:32).

Louise Grings Champlin
Matthew Champlin
April 2012

PREPARATION FOR MISSIONARY SERVICE

Only a sinner saved by grace! Only a sinner saved by grace!
This is my story, to God be the glory.
I'm only a sinner, saved by grace!

They tell me I was born of the flesh in the little railroad town of Burwell, Nebraska, United States of America on the sixteenth day of December 1892. I was present at the time but remember nothing of it.

I was born again, or born of the Spirit, in the same town some time about the year 1902. I can't remember just when it was, but I was very much present on the occasion, and I vividly remember it was in an old-time Methodist revival. The preacher had given the invitation each night for sinners to come forward and give their hearts to the Lord Jesus. Other boys had gone forward, but I had not done so. They came and asked me to go forward, but still I held off till the last night of the meetings. I was scared lest the door of salvation should be shut, and I left outside. Praise God for his loving wooing Spirit, I went forward and knelt down at the mourners' bench and was saved.

Young Herbert Grings

The next day going home from school I told my schoolmates of my conversion and rebuked the Britt girls because they said they believed in dancing. I knew it was wrong to dance because my home had been broken up and my mother was divorced from my father largely because of the dance.

I have a faint recollection of those "shin-digs" and "hoe-downs" in some country farm house when my mother would leave me as a boy of two or three years old lying on a bench while she "saluted your partners, turn to the left; swing 'em on the corner," etc., to the stomping and sawing of one or two fiddles.

Well, my schoolmates laughed and ridiculed me for the stand I took for Jesus. I cried and went and told the old gray-headed Congregational minister, Rev. Mr. Stocking, whose parsonage and church were nearest to my home, about it. He comforted me and said, "Well, Herbert, we have to suffer persecution if we serve the Lord Jesus."

I attended the Congregational Sunday School; and some time later, the Rev. Mr. Stocking asked me to come to a Wednesday night meeting and be baptized. I said I would like to be baptized but that day I had earned a ticket distributing handbills for a vaudeville show and I had to go to the show.

If he had condemned the show and told me to give it up, he probably would have caused me to stumble in my Christian life. The command is not, "Give up something and be baptized," but, "Believe and be baptized." He was a wise old minister and he said, "I'll tell you what you do, Herbert; you come to the meeting, and I will baptize you first, and then you can go to the show."

So I went to the meeting, and he explained to the people that I had earned a ticket for the show and therefore he would baptize me first so I could go. He called me to the front and sprinkled some water on my head in the name of the Father and the Son and the Holy Ghost, and I went to the show. But did I enjoy it? I'll say NO! The show quit me. I didn't quit the show. That open confession of the Lord Jesus in baptism separated me from the world. Although I often went to shows and even ushered in a theater to earn money when I was in business college, I never found satisfaction in going to the show like I did in attending church.

I was accepted as a member of the Congregational church, but I attended the Christian and Methodist churches as I grew up and moved with my mother from place to place. In later years, the Epworth League had a great influence upon my life, and I can also remember BYPU (Baptist Young People's Union).

Then when I was a Yeoman in the U.S. Navy, 1910-1914, Mrs. Chapman, the wife of the Presbyterian minister of Berkeley, California, invited some of us sailors to her home and took us to C.E. (Christian Endeavor) meetings. The C.E. Union of California was a powerful organization in those days. Their yearly state convention caused many young people to dedicate their lives for Christian service.

Herbert in Naval Uniform in San Diego

I was elected as Floating Christian Endeavor (FCE) Superintendent and helped with the meetings on board ships at San Diego harbor. When I was in Bible Institute at BIOLA, I raised money to place libraries of Christian books on three or four of the big warships.

Chief Machinist Mate Jay Walker, Sgt. Paul Goss of the U.S. Marines, and many others on those warships had given their hearts to the Lord Jesus. Instead of a "sweetheart in every port," we had a "mother in every port."

Mother Chapman and Mother Walker were two of them. Mother Chapman gave me a fine leather-bound Scofield Bible, the first Bible I remember having for my own. Seeing another Chief Yeoman on board the *USS Maryland* reading "Christian Science with Key to the Scriptures" when I was Captain's Writer on that ship, I became bold to read my new Scofield Bible openly. And that brings me to my consecration and call to life service for the Lord Jesus.

THE GREAT DECISION

In the last year of my four-year enlistment, I was transferred to the torpedo boat destroyer *Truxtun*. One night as we were tied up to the dock in San Diego harbor and most of the crew had gone ashore on liberty and everything was quiet on board, I was sitting in my little office reading my Bible and the Lord spoke to my heart, "Choose now whether you are going to try to be Paymaster's Clerk or follow me." Thank God he gave me grace to turn my back on a U.S. Navy career and kneel down there on that torpedo boat and dedicate my life to Him.

From that time on I never turned back. When I was given my honorable discharge with recommendation for reenlistment, at Mare Island Navy Yard, Vallejo, California on September 5, 1914, I headed straight for BIOLA, to which Mother Chapman had recommended me after she knew of my decision for Christian life service.

I arrived at the Bible Institute just before the fall term opened. I had saved up $700 or more from my pay in the Navy, so I could pay all my expenses. Oh, what a new and glorious life opened up to me as the young men and young women, three hundred of them, gathered in for the fall term, and I became acquainted with them! All of them were dedicated to the Lord Jesus and had one purpose, to know Him and make Him known.

As the classes opened up and we began to study Chapter Summary, Bible Doctrine, Synthesis, Homiletics, Personal Work, Song Leading, etc., how my spiritual life grew; and my burden for lost souls increased!

In studying Bible Doctrine, and especially the book of Acts, I became convinced that baptism by immersion in water was the way John the Baptist and all the Lord's apostles performed it. Therefore I was not satisfied with my Congregational sprinkling. I went to a meeting in Los Angeles where people were being converted and baptized, and a Baptist minister immersed me. That gave me a clear conscience that I had never had before on that subject. Nobody could question my being baptized in the right way because I was both sprinkled and immersed by an authorized Baptist minister. When people ask me what is my church, I tell them like Dr. Torrey did, "I am a Metho-Presby-Gational-Aptist."

Giving out tracts, testifying in street meetings and streetcar barns, became a joy and satisfaction to me. Then I was assigned to preach in a gospel mission hall. My first sermon was from Genesis 22, and so I was launched to be a preacher of the gospel to the ends of the earth.

While I was in the Navy I had begun to make payments on a house and lot in East San Diego. I had a sweetheart in Alliance, Nebraska, and intended to get married and put my wife there while I pursued my Navy career, but when I dedicated my life to the Lord Jesus, my sweetheart turned and married another fellow. The real estate agent had sold me mortgaged property, so I eventually lost my house and lot. However, I spent the summer vacation from BIOLA there and canvassed nearly the whole of East San Diego, street by street with gospel literature, wall mottoes, etc. I had a weekly Bible study class. One of the members was Frances Stotsky, a Jewish young lady. She was converted, married a shipmate of mine, and joined the Brethren church in Long Beach.

During my last year in BIOLA, I joined the Fishermen's Club, an organization of young men led by Daddy Horton. We met every Monday night for supper together and Bible study afterwards. I can still remember Daddy Horton's message on the text, "Woe is unto me, if I preach not the gospel!" He stretched out his hand over our heads and said, "Oh, that I could put some of that woe upon you, young men!" Truly it fell upon me. I cannot look upon a crowd of people without wanting to preach to them.

One of the members of the Fishermen's Club was Tom Hannay. He went out to preach the gospel to the natives of British East Africa (later Kenya). He became ill with the fever and died there. The call came to us, "Who is going to take his place?" I immediately volunteered. We had an African prayer band in the Institute, and I joined that. A lady who attended these prayer meetings gave me a dollar bill; later it was stolen from me along with my suitcase. She prayed the Lord to multiply it a thousand fold.

I heard Helen and Christine Suderman tell of their work under the Presbyterian board in French Cameroons, West Africa, but I finally made my application to the Africa Inland Mission. They did not give me an immediate answer. When I graduated from BIOLA in June 1916, I still had no word from the mission board, so I decided to take the first opportunity that was offered to get out and preach the gospel.

MOUNTAIN MISSIONARY WORK

I had a telephone call from Daddy Horton. He asked me if I would be willing to go out in Sunday School work in the mountains of Mendocino County, California. I told him I was willing. He asked me how soon I could be ready to go? I said, "In about two hours." He said, "You are just the man we are looking for."

George Wicker and his wife took me in their car to Ukiah, California and introduced me to members of the board they had organized between the Methodist and Christian churches to sponsor a work among the mountain people in the redwood forests of Mendocino County. They gave me a horse and $40 a month, and I started out with an extra shirt and pair of socks in one side of my saddlebags, Bible and gospel literature in the other.

I found some wild folks on those mountain trails. One man had been a criminal in some Eastern state and had come to these mountains to escape the law. He said I could talk about anything but religion in his house. However, his wife and daughter took pity on me and fed me and gave me a place to sleep. Later, they attended the meetings I held in a little schoolhouse. I visited their log cabin again one night, and in came some young men and women from the neighborhood. We all sat and talked for a while in the light of the blazing logs in the wide fireplace. Then the old man got out his fiddle, and they began to dance on the rough slab floor of the log cabin. I sat on a bench just big enough for two. Some one had to sit down beside me at the end of each dance. I didn't fail to talk to that person about his soul's salvation, so everyone got the gospel personally before midnight when they went home.

Some of the young people and children were converted in

the meetings, and the lady schoolteacher took charge of the Sunday School we organized. The houses were far apart, and I never visited more than three or four houses in a day. One time I followed a steep trail back on a mountain ridge and found a neat and pretty little log cabin with a nice glass window. I knocked, but no one answered.

I looked in at the window and there on the table under the lamp stand was a note left by the young wife for her husband. I did not have to read it to know what it said. It probably read something like this, "Bill, I am tired of your going off and leaving me alone for days at a time. If you like the drink shop and those girls down there at the station better than me, you can have them. I'm going back to mother, and don't come and ask me to return to you, for I won't do it!"

She had written the note, put the house neatly in order and then mounted her saddle pony and rode away, only an hour or so before I arrived. If she had only waited an hour or two more I might have been a help in saving that marriage from being broken up.

At Covelo, at one end of the wide and beautiful valley, I found one family with nineteen children, and at the other end, a family of twenty-one. I was able to organize them into a Sunday School. Later, a Free Methodist preacher formed them into a church. He also ministered at the Indian reservation nearby.

After nearly a year of riding my horse over these mountain trails, holding meetings and organizing Sunday Schools, the church board in Ukiah wrote me that I would have to turn in my horse and quit as they had no more money to support me. I told them they could have their horse, which was dragging her hind hoofs from over much riding, but I was not going to quit. I returned the horse to Judge Thompson and took my saddle bags on my shoulder and continued going about on foot among the mountain people, until one day I received a letter from the Africa Inland Mission saying I was accepted for service in the Belgian Congo and to come at once to Los Angeles.

They sent me no money, and I had no funds in hand for the trip, but in the same mail came a letter from the leader of a

Christian Endeavor society which I had organized, saying they felt that the Lord wanted them to help pay my expenses. They enclosed a check for $10 which paid my way to San Francisco. My father was working in that city painting automobiles. I went to see him. He was glad to know that I was going to be a missionary in Africa. I said nothing to him about money, but when I left he gave a $10 gold piece which paid my way to Los Angeles.

At Los Angeles, I went to the Bible Institute and inquired if there was any mail for me, not expecting there would be after a year's absence from there, but the clerk looked in the box, and there was a letter for me which someone had sent in hopes that it would reach me at that address.

The letter contained a check for money enough to pay my board and room until I was formally accepted as a member of the Africa Inland Mission and sent to the Headquarters of the mission in Brooklyn, NY. One test by the mission board of my willingness to work was to clear a vacant lot of weeds on a hot day. I successfully passed the test.

The draft for Word War I was on at that time, and I had to report to the enlistment officer. When I stepped on the scales, I weighed only 114 pounds, after my strenuous running about in the hot weather of Brooklyn. The officer said, "Go back, boy; we don't want you; you are too light!" So the Lord saved me and several other young men at the same time from being taken over to Germany and perhaps killed, and sent us to Africa instead.

CONGO BOUND

At San Francisco, the Devil had put a woman in my path to hinder me from going to Africa. She was then separated from her husband, and I was trying to help her and her old mother spiritually. She insisted that the Lord had told her, "Separate me Barnabas and Saul for the work to which I have called them." She was Barnabas, and I was Saul! She still wrote to me at Brooklyn; but brother Dinwiddie, one of the mission board members, enabled me to shake her off and keep my face set for

Africa.

Then, a young lady, Miss Eve, president of a Christian Endeavor society in Brooklyn where I spoke at their meetings a time or two, became very friendly to me; and people began talking about "Adam and Eve." Again I determined not to let any love affair hinder me from going to Africa, and dropped her friendship.

On the way to Africa, the ship stopped at St. Lucia to take on coal. I went ashore for a quiet walk on a green and pleasant path back from the town. A pretty creole girl met me. We were alone, and all smiles and blushes she said, "Hello, where are you going, mister? Let's have a little kiss."

I told her she should repent of her sins and receive the Lord Jesus as her Savior. She was greatly surprised and asked me if I was a priest. I spent no further time talking with her but pressed a Gospel of John into her hand and hurried back to the ship, thanking the Lord for saving me from another snare of the devil to keep me from going to Africa.

In June 1917, Dr. C. E. Hurlburt, Director of the AIM (Africa Inland Mission), had been used of the Lord to gather together in Brooklyn, NY, forty-six young men and women and married couples from Bible institutes and colleges throughout the land to drive a chain of mission stations from Kasengu on the east border of the Congo to Lake Chad in French Equatorial Africa. The first party of seventeen left for Africa on the British freight and passenger boat, the *City of Athens*, and got through the mines and submarines within sight of Cape Town, when the boat struck a mine and sunk in a few minutes.

All of the AIM missionaries were saved in the lifeboats but with much suffering before a tug came out from the harbor and picked them up. Of course, they lost all their outfits and baggage, but Christian people in Cape Town helped them out. I was sorry I was not in the party when it left; but when we heard of the sinking of the ship, I thanked the Lord for holding me back.

The second party of twenty-five missionaries with the General Director, Dr. Hurlburt, left on the British ship *City of*

Calcutta. They had been at sea only a week or so when the coalbunkers took fire and threatened the destruction of the ship. The missionaries prayed and the fire was brought under control, and the ship put in to a South American port where she was reconditioned and proceeded to Cape Town without further accident. Again I had been left behind and thanked the Lord for sparing me the hardship those missionaries suffered.

But why had I been held back? It was quite a while before I learned why. It was because the Lord wanted me to go in the last little party of four: two young ladies, Margaret Moore and Ruth G. Fuller, another young man, Fay W. Tyler and myself, chaperoned by a Brethren missionary couple, Mr. and Mrs. Hold.

Miss Fuller had a seat by me at the table in the mission home dining room. In that way we became somewhat acquainted. I lacked a sun helmet in my outfit. Without my knowing it she bought me one. After the loss of my "first love," when I was in the Navy, and my experience with those other women, I had fully made up my mind not to be turned aside by any feminine loveliness but to keep steadfastly on for Africa.

Our little party of four left Brooklyn on the British ship *City of Lahore* and made the trip of twenty-one days safely through to Cape Town without accident. We caught up with the other party and went on to Durban and Mombasa as fast as war conditions would permit us to get passage on government-commandeered boats. At the AIM headquarters station Kijabe, near the city of Nairobi, British East Africa, most of us were quartered in the Rift Valley Academy for white children. The cornerstone of the Academy had been laid by ex-president Theodore Roosevelt when he made his hunting expedition to Africa.

At Kijabe, the wife of one of the married couples became ill with the fever and died, so one of the first things I had to do on reaching Africa was to help with a missionary's funeral. Likewise, there were two other missionaries' funerals when I got to Congo. In Los Angeles, I had volunteered to take the place of Tom Hannay who died in British East Africa. Now I was brought face to face with the fact that death was a present possibility here in Africa for new missionaries.

EARLY MISSIONARY SERVICE IN CONGO

We had to break up into small parties of ten to twelve to go on by train and truck to Lake Albert on the Congo frontier. This time I was sent in the first party with Jack Litchman, a converted Jew, and other young men to help build houses for the women missionaries when they arrived. I was among the last to leave the U.S., but among the first to enter Congo, according to the promise, the "first shall be last, and the last shall be first."

On the way out, I had studied Swahili, the language into which Dr. David Livingstone had translated the Scriptures and which Henry M. Stanley used in his explorations of East Africa and in the Congo. Therefore, I could talk with chiefs and headmen who knew that language. This was a great help to me in getting started to preach the gospel almost immediately.

We crossed Lake Albert on a British steamboat which put down on the Congo shore among the naked savages and left us there. Fred Lanning came down from his station at Kasengu, bringing some of his mission boys and men to help us carry our baggage and climb up the steep mountain trail three or four hours to the station. The Belgian Administrateur Territorial had given Mr. Lanning some help in building a row of mud and thatched dormitories sufficient for us all to crowd in and set up the camp equipment which was in our outfits.

I had my Navy hammock and swung it under the eaves of the mission house for a time. We all had to do our own cooking. One fellow tried using a tallow candle to grease his frying pan. When the ladies heard of it, they stopped him and gave him some native sem-sem oil.

The Alur language, Doalur, was reduced to writing. I began studying Doalur and within a few weeks was able to make myself understood pretty well. One of the Alur hymns, set to the tune of "Long, Long Ago," was, *"Mungu amaro danu mumbe, Emio Wode ni botho gin. Negato mu yio ebito ungo, ento, ebedo ku kwo."* (God loves people much, He gave his Son to save them. The person who believes will die not, but abide with life.)

At this time occurred the death of the wife of missionary

John Buijse. We young men made the bamboo coffin and carried it down to the station near the lake and helped bury her body. Lack of salt and poor nourishment was partly the cause of her death.

Station sites in the various tribes had been chosen by a previous exploration party of missionaries, and as soon as possible the General Director began sending out the parties of two's, four's and five's to those sites. Jack Litchman, the Jew, and I were assigned to go with Andy Uhlinger and wife to the south end of Lake Albert and open a station among the Bahema and Babira people at Bogoro.

Miss Ruth Fuller told the General Director that she had a "reason" for wanting to go also and be the teacher in the mission school. He kindly sent her. She had a good bicycle and went with Uhlinger's caravan. Jack and I and Field Director Lanning came later, as it was very difficult to raise caravans of porters to carry all the equipment and baggage.

It was an exhilarating trip of five long days hiking along with the caravan through many big villages, past the Kilo gold mines and Bunia to Bogoro. We camped in the government rest house. Mr. Uhlinger chose a beautiful site on the high escarpment overlooking Lake Albert, and we began building a mission house for him and his wife. In years past there had been a government post at Bogoro. They had built many sun-dried brick houses. The bricks in the foundations of these houses were still good. We dug them out with mattock and shovel, hitched ourselves to an abandoned gold mine wagon and hauled them to the station site.

We built and studied the language and preached, and the women started a school with the native children. Within six months or so, we not only had the frame of the house up, but a native school and regular gospel meetings going. Then Field Director Fred Lanning came along and sent Jack and I off to open another station among the Balendu people at Blukwa, seven thousand feet above sea level in the Balega mountains.

The tribes were at war with each other. The men of one tribe would carry our baggage up to the border of the next tribe and put it down and go back. Then we would have to hunt and talk and pray to get another caravan to come out into the wilderness and pick up our baggage and carry it on for the next stage of the "safari." Jack had to leave me and go for three days to the nearest government post, Djugu, to get a load of the small coins called *makutas* and *catawanjis*, to pay these porters.

The porters had gone back and left me alone on a bare hilltop with the baggage. I just threw myself down with my face to the ground and prayed for a while. I heard some footsteps and looked up. There was a government headman dressed in the official shirt and short pants.

Said he, "Have these *bashenzi* (savages) gone off and left you again? I'll fix them." With that, he shouldered his muzzle-loading rifle and marched away to the nearest village and soon returned with sufficient porters to carry, by relays, all our baggage to the village of the great Bahema chief Blukwa, who ruled over the Balendu tribe as well as the Bahemas.

THE BLUKWA STATION

The Bahemas were a superior tribe of people and considered rich because they owned many head of cattle and lived mainly by trading beef, milk, and butter. The Balendus were an agricultural people, raising kaffir corn, millet, beans and sweet potatoes. They also had many head of fat-tailed sheep and goats which they used mainly for buying wives.

The Bahema man had to pay three or four head of cattle for a Bahema woman, but he could usually buy a Balendu woman for only one cow. Many of the Bahema men took Balendu women for wives. Of course, their children spoke the language of their mothers, which caused the Bahema tribe to degenerate or at least to become more like the Balendus.

The Bahema women wore thoroughly tanned and softened skins of cows or calves, with innumerable strings of beads and cowry shells. The men wore long flowing *kanzus* made of yards of cloth draped over their shoulders and reaching down to their feet. They usually carried long spears.

The Balendu women wore an abbreviated apron, beads and plenty of paint. The men wore tanned and softened-by-chewing sheepskin or goatskin breechclouts passed between the legs and supported from the waist by a fiber cord or rawhide strap. They painted their arms and legs with charcoal mixed with oil from the castor bean which they grew for the purpose. They chiseled their teeth sharp like a dog's teeth and twisted their kinky hair into pigtails. They cut cicatrices in cheeks and forehead.

The men always carried short bows and arrows with barbed iron points. In time of war, they carried tough woven fiber shields and spears with a slender shaft ten or twelve feet long. When they cast the spear at an enemy, they would let it slide through their hand to the end and then draw it back quickly for another throw.

The old chief Blukwa received me in a friendly manner and invited me into his great round grass house which was twenty feet high in the center and twenty-five or thirty feet in diameter, with two or three partitions for his many wives. Blukwa had royal blood in his veins, and he ruled with wisdom and power over the people. He did not look directly at me but turned his face sidewise and glanced at me from the corner of his eyes. When he did so, his eyes seemed to flash fire like a leopard's eyes. I always felt that he was possessed of a spirit that was more than human, perhaps one of the powers of the Prince of Darkness. The government officials had built three-room rest houses in most of the villages for white people. In that manner the Lord's promise in Mark 10:30 was fulfilled, that whosoever leaves houses or lands, etc., for the sake of the gospel, shall receive a hundred fold now in this time.

When my partner Jack arrived from the government post with a load of those *makutas* and *catawanjis*, we were ready to begin hiring men to build our mission house. We talked with Chief Blukwa and told him we had come to tell his people about the great God in heaven who had sent his Son Jesus Christ to save them from their sins and take them to heaven when they died. We explained that we would make a school and teach the children how to read God's book. He seemed very pleased with our talk and promised to call the men we needed to work for us.

About that time I was confined to my camp cot with an attack of malarial fever. Jack went out and chose a site for the mission station on the far side of a swamp near the forest-covered mountain Wagu. It was too far and too inaccessible from the villages. We had no more than got the frame of our house up when the Field Director Mr. Lanning came along and moved us out to an ideal site on a long grassy ridge with villages on all sides. We moved the frame of our first house and completed it. After that our progress in building was slow because no men wanted to work. We were able to hire a couple of boys to bring water and firewood and help us with our cooking. We studied the language with them and began to reduce it to writing.

The Batha (Balendu language) is a most peculiar language, being completely monosyllabic. The five vowels, *a e i o u*, are all words, and each one has several meanings. Then you have *ba be bi bo bu*, *da de di do du, fa fe fi fo fu*, right on through the alphabet. Then you have some words without vowels: *dz ngr drdr tsz nz*. That is the language, not hard to learn or pronounce indeed; but the difficult part is to get the order and construction of those words into grammatical sentences. *A bu da ma tho*: give water me for (to). *Yesu u na ke ka go nba*: Jesus believing person will be saved yes. *Nza u Yesu na ke ka go nza*: the not believing Jesus person will be saved not. The language has no infinitive: to go, to work, etc. *Ma zi ma ra ra*: I want I go going. *Ma zi ma nji nji*; I want I work work. *Ma ka ni be nza*; I will you see not; but, *Ma ka be-ni nza*: I will be seen not.

Of the six languages I learned during my twenty years in Congo, I think I mastered the Batha best. I translated the entire New Testament into that language, besides Old Testament stories, hymns, primer and school material.

A MOVE AND A BRIDE

After about six months at the Blukwa station, I was ordered by the General Director to go to the Aru station on the Uganda border. They had opened so many stations that there were not enough missionaries to man them all. They sent Mr. and Mrs.

Mount over the Uganda border to take charge of the Aru station and eventually left me alone to hold down the Aru station without even a cat for a companion.

I got so discouraged that I decided to leave and go back to British East Africa and search for a wife. I was making a round table and needed a vine to nail around the edge. When that was done, I said to myself I will go to the village and call porters to carry my baggage and start out. I went down into the forest and found a big vine hanging straight down from a tree. Just what I wanted! I climbed up the tree and cut down the vine. When I climbed up the tree, there were no ants in sight; but when I started down, there were hundreds of big pincher ants coming up to attack me.

I climbed back up the tree to escape and then tried to jump across to another tree like the monkeys do; but my hands slipped off the limb and I fell about twenty-five feet, striking a stump in my right side and breaking a rib. To breathe was like stabbing a knife in my side. All I could do was to lie there and gasp and groan for about an hour, but as there was no one to come to my help, I crawled back to the house and went to bed for three or four days, only crawling out long enough to cook some oatmeal porridge or whatever I had to eat. Thus it was the Lord kept me from running away like Jonah did. Word of it finally reached the General Director, and he ordered me to headquarters at Aba to help in his office.

But I wasn't any more content at Aba than I had been at Aru. I tried to run away again, but the porters I had ordered went to the General Director. He called me and asked what was the "big idea?" I had to confess that I wanted to go to British East Africa and seek for a wife.

Kind, old gray-headed Dr. Hurlburt put his arm around my shoulder and said, "Grings, the Lord wanted to give you a wife long ago, but you wouldn't take the hint. That schoolteacher at Bogoro (Miss Ruth G. Fuller) thinks the world of you." Maybe he knew it, but I didn't; so I wrote a letter to her to find out.

There were no cars, airplanes or trains to carry mail in that part of the Congo, only foot messengers; and it took nearly three weeks for that letter to go from Aba in the northeast corner of the Congo to Bogoro at the south end of Lake Albert. Oh, those weeks were about the longest weeks in my life, but when the answer came, it was all right. She wrote, "Dear Boy, Oh, I have been waiting so long for this letter." The Lord had a wife ready and waiting for me. It was I who was slow in finding it out.

With porters to carry my baggage, it was a ten days "safari" from Aba to Bogoro. I was in such a hurry to get there that once I rode far ahead of my porters on my bicycle, and at night they did not catch up with me at the rest house where I stopped, so I had to sleep on a bamboo table without blanket or mosquito net. I didn't sleep much because there were myriads of malarial mosquitoes, along with the cold and hard bed to keep me awake.

As a result of this haste, I was delayed at Ter Akara mission station with an attack of malarial fever which lasted four days. How true is the saying, "Haste makes waste."

Ruth Fuller's Graduation Picture

But at last I got there. Within a week's time, I and the schoolteacher lady, a 1910 graduate of Moody Bible Institute, agreed to get married as soon as we could do so. That didn't seem to be very soon, as it would take about a year to get in French all the legal documents required by the government to be married in the Belgian Congo.

But love and prayer found a way. We joined a big caravan with a missionary bachelor as chaperon and went over into Uganda to the Aru mission station. After two weeks, on December 3, 1919, we were married under British law by the Commissioner. We rode our bicycles to the post, dressed in our ordinary travel clothes. Two witnesses, Mr. and Mrs. C. H. Mount, went with us. The District Commissioner asked me, "Will you have this woman for your wife?" I replied, "I will." He asked Ruth, "Will you have this man for your husband?" She replied, "Yes, Sir!" He said, "Sign here." We signed the wedding certificate, and the witnesses signed after us. Then the D. C. pronounced us man and wife and read the law that if we ever were divorced and married again we would be guilty of adultery.

We had a literal *honeymoon*. Ruth needed some dental work done before we went to open our new station among the Balendus. The nearest dentist was General Director Hurlburt at Aba. It was too hot to travel by day, so we went by *moonlight*, riding our bicycles leisurely along ahead of our porters and faithful cook boys. The fragrance and felicity of that honeymoon will remain with me to the end of my days. Certainly there was some danger in traveling by night. We passed through a country where the fierce wild buffaloes wandered about by night. Once we had to walk and push or carry our bicycles over hundreds of holes in the path made by the feet of elephants of two tons or more in weight, which had recently passed that way.

THE LINGA STATION

With the dental work done at Aba, our honeymoon was ended, and we set out on the long "safari" back to Balendu territory where the General Director assigned us to open a new station at Linga village, one long day's tramp over thirteen ridges and ravines north of the Blukwa. We arrived at a retired Belgian government official's plantation, Mons. Francois, on the border of the Balendu and Alur tribes. I left my wife there while I went to explore the Balendu tribe. I said to her, "If I find two large villages within a day's walking distance of each other, I will consider that as the Lord's place for us."

Actually, I found five big villages averaging three hundred people each, with a splendid station site about midway between and a little off from the government road on a wide ridge sloping down from Mount Pli. The headman of Linga village invited me to come, and I hastened back to bring my wife. Mons. Francois helped us raise a caravan of porters to carry my wife in a *tipoi* (chair swung on bamboo poles), and all our household equipment and baggage, and away we went to open Linga, my second station in the Balendu tribe.

We arrived among a great crowd of naked (except for loincloth or apron) men, women and children who had never before seen a white woman. My wife spoke three languages: Kingwana, Doalur and Orahuma. I spoke Kingwana, Doalur, Lingala, and a little Batha. Therefore, we were able to talk to the people and, with an intelligent headman as interpreter, to preach the gospel of our Lord Jesus Christ.

We camped in the government rest house, and I went every day to clear the station site and build a house. I couldn't get many men to work for me, so at first I built just one round mud and wattle house fifteen feet in diameter with one door and two windows. The red mud in the wall was not yet dry when we moved in, but it was our own home, and we were as happy as any birds in their nests could be. We had to do our cooking on an open fire outside, and my wife put her shining pots into the fire, never to shine again.

The witchdoctor began to oppose us and warn the young boys not to work for us or come to our school. One report they circulated was that we had a hole under our table, and if a boy came near to bring us food from the outside fireplace, we would catch him and throw him into the hole and eat him.

At first, we had to cut our firewood and carry our water from the spring in the ravine ourselves; but one day a fine young man named Jilo came to our door and said he wanted to work for us. I gladly put a bush knife and hoe into his hands and told him to clear the path to our water spring. He worked diligently for two or three hours and came back saying the path was cleared. I inspected his work which was very satisfactory. Then I tried to tell him the story of God's creating the world, but he seemed very nervous and asked me to pay him so he could go to the village and buy something to eat. I gave him a *catawanji*, the twenty *centimos* coin with a hole in the center. The Balendus delighted to put these coins on a string and tie them about their waists or necks.

He took his pay and went away quickly. He came back the next day and worked and got another *catawanji*. This time he listened a little better to my Bible story, but hurried away to the village as soon as I would let him go. He came back on the third and fourth days and worked. He brought poles and thatch grass for a little cookhouse I was building, and on the fifth day it was done. He listened very intently to my story of Jesus opening the eyes of the blind man, and I persuaded him to kneel down with me while I talked to this invisible Lord Jesus with him. Then I asked him if he would not like to make his bed in this new cookhouse and stay with us all the time. He fearfully accepted.

Little by little, we learned Jilo's story. He was a son of the sub-chief who lived down by the lake on the east side of the mountains from us. His father was a Bahema but his mother was Balendu. He spoke both languages, and Kingwana as well. Since my wife knew Orahuma, the Bahema language, she talked to him in that language which delighted him very much and seemed to relieve his fear of us. He said he was to inherit the chieftainship when his old father died, but his brothers were jealous of him and threatened to kill him. He heard of the *muzungu* (white man) at Linga's village, but they told him that the *muzungu* bewitched and killed people. He had a great desire in his heart to go and see this white man but was afraid that he would die if he did so. However, he was more afraid of dying at the hands of his envious brothers, so he made up his mind to take the chance and came to us. After his first day's work for us, he went to the village and passed the night fearfully, expecting some calamity to happen to him. But nothing happened, so he came the second and third and fourth days, and now he was willing to stay and be our cook boy.

My wife taught him Bible stories in the Orahuma, more clearly than I could with my then limited knowledge of Batha. Then one day he knelt down with us and gave his heart to the Lord Jesus. Oh, what a new creature in Christ Jesus. He was our first convert. He began to use his influence to bring boys from the village to work for us and learn letters in the school.

One day after Jilo had been with us for two or three months he said to me, "Teacher, I want to go back to my village down by the lake and to bring my brothers here to learn the words of God." We were fearful of what might happen to him, but after prayer and counsel we sent him away. He was gone a week or ten days, and -- wonder of wonders! -- when he came back, two of those younger brothers who had threatened to take his life were with him. It was not long before they were converted; and then came the break, and boys and girls and men and women began to come to our meetings from far and near. Others were converted, and the school increased greatly.

One of the saddest sights in these villages was the large number of people with great tropical ulcers on their feet and legs. Also, the burrowing flea or jigger often ate off, or caused to rot off, the toes especially of the children. We treated these cases with what disinfectant and healing sulfur powder we had, and many were cured. One woman crawled on her hands and knees two hours from and to her village for many days to have me doctor her ulcerated feet. I made a charge of five or ten ears of corn, or some eggs, for treating large ulcers, but this did not stop them from coming.

THE KBA-NDRO-MA (RETHI) STATION

When I sent a report to mission headquarters of the great opportunity for medical work in this tribe, they responded by sending Dr. Charles Trout and family to take over the Linga station and sent Ruth and me a day's "safari" further north to open my fourth mission station on the border of the Balendu, Alur and Bakebu tribes, near the village of Kba-ndro-ma (they hate me). Later the station was called "Rethi" after the name of the low flat-topped hill on which it was built.

The men from these villages were more willing to work; therefore I was able to build a fairly comfortable three-room mud and wattle house. To pay the workmen and buy our food, Ruth often sewed up strips of cloth for a girdle around the waist. The men supported their loincloths with a twisted fiber string around the waist, which often made sores on the hips; therefore they were very glad to work a day for one of these soft cloth girdles which they called *ru-mbi* (cloth string). The mission treasurer sent us a check, but we couldn't cash it in the jungles. We had to send it back and get along by trading *ru-mbis*, empty food tins, needles, etc., for food supplies and to pay the workmen.

Our house had no wooden doors, only drop mats woven from the elephant grass. Rats began to infest our house. I set traps for them. In the night when I heard the trap go "Snap!" I would get up, take the dead rat out of the trap, throw it outside of the door, set the trap and go back to bed. In the morning, I looked for the dead rat outside, but it was not there. The next night after a rainstorm, I threw another dead rat outside the door and went back to bed. When I looked for it in the morning, it was gone, but there in the mud just in front of the door were large leopard tracks! Needless to say, I threw no more dead rats out in front of the door and made haste to get something more substantial than a drop mat to close the door.

We had no more than gotten the work nicely started than it became necessary for us to leave our station and go to be with Dr. Trout at Linga station for the birth of our first baby. While we were waiting for that important event, a call came for Dr. Trout to go down the escarpment to Lake Albert in the Alur tribe where a Belgian government official lay gravely sick of the blackwater fever. This would be a safari of five or six days to go and return. In the meantime our baby might be born, and the mother die in childbirth. God gave Dr. Trout wisdom to make the difficult decision that, in all due respects, a missionary's wife who could teach school and the Word of God in four native languages had the priority over a government official.

Dr. Trout sent me with remedies and instructions. I made the exhausting trip, first by bicycle as far as I could go with it, then seven thousand feet down the escarpment on foot. Then, with the help of government soldiers, I got porters to carry me by night in a "tipoi" to where the government official lay at death's door, passing much bloody urine, which is one of the effects of the dread blackwater fever. At that time, it was fatal in about nine cases out of ten.

I administered the remedies that Dr. Trout had sent to the official, and then as he had word that Dr. Woodhams of the Ter

Akara mission station was coming to treat him, I was free to return to my wife. By God's good help, I got back before the baby was born. The doctor had not been able to build a hospital at that time; therefore, we stayed in that same little old round house which I built when we first opened the station. Dr. Trout and wife were living in the little mud and wattle cookhouse which Jilo helped me build. Thanks be to God, through the skillful assistance of Dr. Trout, after four hours of hard labor, on the morning of November 15, 1920, Ruth gave birth to our first son whom we named Robert Ernest.

We joyfully returned to our Kba-ndro-ma (Rethi) station with our new baby and went ahead with language study, teaching, medical work and itinerating with bicycles to the surrounding villages. The medical work soon developed to such an extent that the mission transferred Dr. Trout to open his hospital at Rethi and sent us back to Linga.

To me, the village work was more important than the station work. We closed up the house and went out with a tent and preached for weeks at a time in all the big villages round about. The baby was a great attraction. They had never before seen a white woman and her baby. We were constantly in a crowd and could preach the gospel from morning to night. At times I preached ten or fifteen times a day, beginning at break of day and ending up by moonlight at night.

Before the Doctor moved from Linga, Miss Halstead, a missionary down by the lake in the Alur tribe had brought some of the native babies up for treatment for dysentery. There was no place for them to stay but in the cookhouse. Another missionary lady, Miss Bertha Peterson, sweetheart of Titus Johnson at the Blukwa station, was staying with the doctor till they could get married. She caught the dysentery from those native children, and in spite of all the doctor could do to save her life, she died.

We made a coffin of split bamboo and buried her in a beautiful grassy plot back of the mission station. That was the third missionary woman I had helped to bury since my arrival in Africa. Titus was brokenhearted. Soon he and Jack Litchman were transferred from the Blukwa station, and Ruth and I sent there.

Before we moved however, we went to Dr. Trout's hospital at Rethi where our second son, Roy Gerald, was born on January 20, 1922. This was just at the time of the influenza epidemic which mysteriously dropped down in many parts of the world and killed thousands of people. Many sick people came to Dr. Trout. I caught the infection and was very sick. Ruth had taken the newborn baby and gone to Ter Akara, so escaped being sick.

BACK TO THE BLUKWA STATION

Some time later we arrived at the Blukwa station and took over the work there. Titus Johnson had built a nice house from local material with a really Swedish touch, having solid wooden doors and window shutters. It had a nice kitchen with iron stove, so Ruth did not have to cook outside on fire stones as before. We lived more comfortably in that house than anywhere we had been before, but we did not let those comforts keep us tied down to the station. I would go out on a preaching trip through the many villages for two weeks. When I came back Ruth would say, "Now it's my turn." She would take the baby carried by two of our schoolboys in a basket tied to a pole and go out for a week or so and teach the women and children in the villages.

Our school and station work increased greatly. At one time, I had 150 boys and men on my payroll. All of this was paid for out of our personal funds. We were trusting the Lord to supply all our needs without promise of pay from anybody. We never asked for funds, and we never went in debt. With the help of my schoolboys, I built our first sun-dried brick house, into which we moved when Miss Love, the single worker, came to help in the schoolwork. She lived in Titus Johnson's house.

One Saturday when I came back from a two-week preaching trip, my wife met me and said excitedly, "Tomorrow you are going to see something that will surprise you. We had a big crowd for church service last Sunday but there will be a bigger crowd this Sunday." Truly it was so. The people began gathering before 7 a.m.; and by 9:30, the church building was packed full, and more were standing outside than were inside.

We had been having sixty or seventy people at the morning service, but there must have been five hundred people in this crowd.

We had trained four or five of the young men to go out and preach the gospel. They walked on the ridges to go to distant villages. Those who opposed the gospel derided these young evangelists, calling them, "*tze-jo-nga-bi-na-kba*," which means "ridge on place walking the men" (ridge-walkers). These young men began bringing in their converts to the station for Sunday morning services, and we seated them in groups in the church. One group would vie with another in standing up and repeating Scripture verses or singing choruses as we called the name of the village from which they came.

Many of these converts were ready for baptism, but in those days I was governed by the general policy of mission boards to keep a convert on probation for a year or two before baptism, instead of obeying the plain command to make disciples, baptizing them and *then* teaching them. Baptism is a test of obedience, and when a new convert steps out and is publicly baptized, it establishes and settles him in the determination to follow the Lord Jesus. Teaching then follows with the Lord's blessing.

Once again it became necessary for us to leave our station and go to the doctor for the birth of our third child. In order to preach the gospel in the most villages on the way, we chose to go three days "safari" to the Bogoro station and then two days further on to Nyangkundi near Irumu, Ituri Province, where Dr. Woodhams was beginning to build his hospital. The hospital was still in the blueprint stage. He let us camp in his new church building. Thus it was that our daughter Elisabeth Charlotte (we called her Bessie), was born in a church on Sunday morning, August 23, 1925. (Of course no meeting was going on!) The Belgian Congo government official gave her a birth certificate for August 25th, but I am sure if one had a 1925 calendar he would find that Sunday was August 23rd.

We always dedicated our babies to the Lord before they were born and then as soon as possible after their birth brought them to the church for a public dedication service, not baptism, in which we promised to teach them the Word of God and lead them to accept the Lord Jesus as their personal Savior.

When we started home we couldn't raise enough porters for a "tipoi" for Ruth, so she took the baby in a cloth swung around her neck and rode her bicycle. I carried our two small sons, Robert and Roy with me on my bicycle. They, and especially the new baby, drew crowds of people to see them in the native villages through which we passed. Ruth probably witnessed to more women on that trip than any before. When we arrived back at the Blukwa station, crowds of people came on Sunday to see the new baby, but Ruth kept her in the house and told them they would first have to attend the church service and afterwards she would bring the baby out for them to see, which she did. In that manner, Bessie, who was born in a church, began to bring people to church when she was a tiny baby, and at the present writing, (November 2, 1963) is still doing so.

We enlarged our church building, but it was soon filled on Sundays, and people stood on the outside. I tried to take a picture of the people after the morning service but couldn't get them all in it. There must have been a thousand people at that service, so mightily did the Holy Spirit move in all those Balendu villages.

We were building neat little sun-dried brick houses for the married couples who lived on our station. One day during a rainstorm lightning struck one of these houses and set the grass roof on fire. I was just coming back from a preaching trip and saw the smoke from a distant village where I had stopped to take shelter from the rain. When I arrived at the station I found that while the native women stood around screaming and wailing, Ruth had to play fireman and go into the burning house and drag out a boy who had been stunned by the lightening.

Because of her faith and courage, the people greatly respected her. Ruth's teaching in the school was much blessed of the Lord. Among those she taught to read and write, and whom I sent out to preach the gospel were Kole, Pitsolo, Tekba, Dzna, Buda, Ravanga and Kekba. One of her students in the school, Ngakba, was a blind man of the Kebu or blacksmith tribe. Of course, he couldn't learn to read, but he memorized Scripture verses and became a faithful believer.

With so many people living on the station whom I had to feed, I tried to raise part of the food. Besides planting beans and corn, which was the principal diet of the natives, I brought in French blue and red potatoes and began planting them. This was new food for them, but they soon learned to like it and carried potato seed to their villages for their fathers and mothers to plant. When Jack and I had opened the station, we planted black wattle trees which grew from seed. As these grew, they not only beautified our station but furnished abundance of seed which the natives carried to their villages and planted. Groves of beautiful trees began springing up on many of the ridges.

SAVED THROUGH JESUS NAME

With the entrance of the gospel, great changes were taking place among these pagan people. When the Belgian government officials first came in, the people would not pay taxes. They shot the black soldiers with poisoned arrows. The soldiers retaliated by shooting with their rifles, man, woman, or child.

One sub-chief revolted and took his people over the mountain and down by the lake on the other side. The government official sent word to him that if he didn't return and build his village on the government road, he was coming to make war on them. When I heard that, I said to my wife, "If he goes down there, he will kill a lot of people." She agreed, and we prayed. Then I took five or six of the schoolboys to carry my folding cot, chop box, and tent and started over the mountain to reach that rebel village.

One thing I did not take was a gun. I never carried a gun in all my travels and that probably saved my life that day because a year or so later some of my converts told me, "Teacher, when you passed through the forest we were hiding behind trees ready to shoot with our poisoned arrows, but when we looked out and saw no soldiers and no gun, just a lone white man, with those young men, we said, 'What kind of a white man is that? Let him go.'" So I went on over the mountain and down the other side, and there on a ridge below was the rebel village. They looked up and saw my white sun helmet and thought it was the government official coming to make war on them. Immediately there was a commotion in that village. The boys drove off the sheep and goats while the women grabbed their pots and fled to the forest. Then the men set fire to their grass huts and scattered to the forest to fight to the finish. I didn't fully realize the danger I was in, but my boys did, and they kept behind me.

I ran down through the clearing shouting, "Don't burn your houses; don't burn your houses." Just then I saw a man crouching behind a log with the arrow drawn taut on his bow. I stood still, expecting to feel that arrow pierce my body, but instead, the Spirit whispered in my heart, "Tell him, 'Don't kill me, I am a man of Jesus.'" I raised my hands above my head and shouted, "*Nzi hwi ma hwi. Ma ku Yesu dza ke!*" I don't think he had ever heard the name of Jesus before, but when I shouted, "*Yesu dza ke*," (Jesus' man), God honored the name and touched the man's heart, and he lowered his bow and arrow. I approached him and said, "Don't fight against the government official, he has guns that can shoot five times. He can kill all of you. Call the people. I want to tell you the words of Jesus." He pressed his cheeks together with his thumb and middle finger and let out a "Ho-o-o-o-lo!" ending the "lo" by snapping the thumb and middle finger sharply through his open mouth.

In response to his call, the warriors came up on all sides of me. They were armed with bows and arrows and spears. They were painted and tattooed; their teeth were chiseled sharp like a dog's teeth; charcoal rubbed into their hair and goat skins for a loincloth. I explained to them that I was not a government official but a Jesus man. I did not come to make war but to tell them the words of God. They were willing to listen, and we went and sat down by the burning embers of their houses which were now completely consumed by the fire. The women and boys came back from hiding in the forest, and I sat for hours and told them the story of creation, the fall, Cain and Abel.

When I told them of Abel's blood sacrifice they said, "We understand that because we always give blood sacrifices to Go."

Who was Go? Was he a good Spirit? No, "*Go ku che.*" (Satan is bad), they said. I asked them what was the name of the good God who had made the earth and sky and sun and moon and all things? The young men hesitated to speak his name, but after some questioning, an old man said, "*Ke ro tho ku Ja.*" (His name is Ja.) There I had the Hebrew name for Jehovah God, preserved in this heathen tribe. Later I found Mosaic rituals like the scapegoat, purification of women and water of cursing, etc.

I slept in my tent that night while the people found what shelter they could around their open fires. The next morning I preached to them again and urged them to submit to the government official and come out and build their village on the government road, and make me a schoolhouse, so I could teach them the words of God.

They agreed to do so, and I went back and told my wife how near she came to being a widow. She said she had prayed fervently for my safety. We knelt down and prayed and praised the Lord again. In less than two weeks, the rebels had submitted to the government, built their village where he ordered, and also built a schoolhouse. I sent one of our best married couples to teach them and soon there were many converts to the Lord Jesus in their village.

As the gospel changed the hearts and lives of the people, there arose a great need for clothing and better ways of living. God provided for that by permitting white men to come in and discover gold even in the little streams where we had washed our clothes. They hired great numbers of the natives to work these mines, Kilo being the central mine. Traders came in with all sorts of European and Asiatic products for sale. It was not long before the goatskin breechclouts and the grass aprons gave way to pants and shirts and dresses. Aluminum pots, cups and dishes took the place of the earthen pots, gourds and calabashes. With the entrance of the gospel, a new era dawned for the Balendu people.

MINISTRY YEARS IN THE USA

After eight years of constant service in the Belgian Congo, the mission board decided it was time to send us back to America. They sent the Whittermores, Baptist missionaries, and Miss Love to relieve us. Brother Whittermore, being a Baptist, had no hesitation in baptizing our two leading couples, Kole and his wife and Pitsolo and his wife. There were numerous other converts who should have been baptized, but we left them in the hands of the new missionaries and started for the U. S. A.

At Kijabe in British East Africa (later Kenya), we were delayed about two months for the birth of our fourth child. In the well-equipped hospital of the Africa Inland Mission, under the care of Dr. Davis, on August 25, 1926, Grant Fuller Grings was born.

Grings Family - 1926

In the meantime, I had been busily occupied in mimeographing our translations of the gospels of Mark and Luke, which I sent to the Congo before we sailed from Mombasa for Kobe on the Japanese freight boat *Mexico Maru*. We had to go deck passage as our funds were very limited. In fact, no funds at all had been sent in for our passage to America. But, the young men Paul Hurlburt and Floyd Pierson, who were in control of the Africa Inland Mission headquarters at Aba upon the retirement of Dr. Charles Hurlburt, had conferred with Andy Uhlinger and appropriated some money from his furlough fund to send us back to the U.S. against our will.

We had to take our own food for the deck passage; and among the other groceries I bought was a case of condensed milk for our new baby. The grocery man sent the things to the ship with Ruth and the four children. I asked him if he had sent the case of milk, and he said he had done so. I was delayed in bringing the rest of our baggage from the mission house in a dilapidated old Model T Ford driven by a tricky Hindu man. The jolly good British customs officer said, "Your Mem-sahib, (Mrs.) has already gone aboard. Get into my boat, and I will send you out to the ship."

The ship had already weighted anchor when I got aboard with the baggage, so there was no time to check the grocery list. The ship steamed out of port into the Indian Ocean, and I went below to get a tin of milk for the baby. I searched in vain for the case of milk. The grocery man had failed to send it with the other things! Seventeen days of ocean voyage ahead, and no milk for the baby! What would we do? Why did the Lord permit such a calamity? If ever I was tempted to doubt the goodness of the Lord, it was then. It took me some time to regain my spiritual equilibrium, but finally I went into a corner and knelt down and told the Lord I would trust him even if the baby died.

Ruth found a big bottle of malted milk in our baggage, such as convalescent patients might eat. This seemed to agree very well with the baby's digestion. When it was gone, we used one or two tins of milk we had in our chop box and kept for him instead of using it on porridge. Then, before the voyage ended, we persuaded the ship's steward to give us some tinned milk from first class. In that way got through to Singapore. Perhaps the malted milk and the strongly diluted tinned milk were better for the baby than if he had had liberal feedings of that evaporated sweetened milk.

From Singapore to Kobe, Japan, the weather was too cold for us to go by deck passage. The steward put us into a second-class compartment with other poor passengers. At Kobe, I went ashore first to seek a place to stay. About the first thing I saw was a sign in English of a real estate office. The agent spoke good English, and I asked him if he had a vacant room to rent. He rented me a big unfurnished upstairs room in a house near the dock, and I brought the family and our baggage ashore. We lived in that room and did our own cooking very cheaply and happily instead of going to an expensive hotel. I also found that printing was very cheap at Kobe and had five hundred copies of a little book of Old Testament stories printed in the Batha and sent to them in Congo before we left for Yokohama to make connections with a ship going to the United States.

I had visited the port of Yokohama in 1912, while I was in the Navy. At that time it was a cluster of bamboo houses with a dilapidated landing pier and customs house. A swarm of rickshaw men pressed upon a stranger calling, "Likshaw, Likshaw!" They would take you trotting all around town for a few sen. The people wore sandals and colorful kimonos. In particular, I remember visiting one of the idol temples. There was a gong and a brass pot at the entrance. I watched an intelligent-looking Japanese man in a beautiful kimono and sandals come up, ring the gong to waken the god, drop some coins into the brass pot, bow low, and make his prayer.

Now, after fourteen years, all things were changed. A Japanese commission had gone around the world and brought back many modern ways of living and building houses. A concrete warehouse took the place of the old wooden ones; and instead of the rickshaw, Yellow Cab taxies, with uniformed chauffeurs met you with, "Taxi, sir. Taxi, sir." There was an electric train to Tokyo with English-speaking conductors, just like in the U.S., and I could pay the fare in U.S. or Japanese money. When I passed the idol temple, an intelligent-looking man was there, dressed in a nice suit with shirt and necktie and patent leather shoes just like in the U.S. His manner of dress was changed, but he rang the same old gong, dropped his coin into the same old pot and made his same old bow and prayer to the same old idol. His manner of living had changed but not his religion.

From Yokohama to San Francisco, California, we again took third class passage in a deck compartment with immigrants and poor people, on the *Shinyo Maru*. When we arrived at Honolulu, some missionaries came on board to visit us and lovingly paid the difference and put us in a big comfortable second class cabin for the rough and tempestuous voyage from there on to San Francisco. I had written to my father telling him when we would arrive, but he was not at the pier to meet us. I inquired at the post office and found my card was still there undelivered as my father had gone away to some other place without leaving a forwarding address.

ITINERATING IN THE STATES

Our wanderings in America are a long and drab story: San Francisco to San Pedro and Los Angeles, with visits to the Church of the Open Door and Bible Institute of Los Angeles. Bobby and Roy had their first experience in kindergarten at San Pedro. My mother came out from Nebraska to live with my father at Stockton, and we went to be with them. Then, I bought Dad's old Chevy truck; and with a trailer to carry the baggage, we started out to find Indians at Gila Bend, Arizona, among whom we could do missionary work. My mother went along.

We did not find Indians at Gila Bend. I sent my mother back to Stockton, and we went on to Prescott, Arizona. We bought a lot there, and I built a temporary house, but we did not stay long. My stepbrothers Harry and Elmer Kipp in Kulm, North Dakota, invited me to come and work in their Chevrolet and Buick agency. I went there with Bobby while Ruth took the other three children and went on to visit her sister in Garrettsville, Ohio.

I received an invitation from evangelist Bob Jones to come and work in the office of his Christian college which he was building at Lynn Haven, Florida. Ruth rejoined me, and we went in another old car with a trailer. I worked in the office for several months and then resigned and gave myself wholly to translating and typing the manuscript of the New Testament in Batha. I sent the manuscript to Blukwa, and eventually the language committee revised it and had it printed in London. This was my final work for the Balendu tribe.

On June 12, 1928, our daughter Louise May was born in Lynn Haven, Florida. We dedicated her to the Lord in the Presbyterian church. The old minister, Reverend Hall, consented to perform the service without the sprinkling baptism of that church. With a wife and five children to support, I sought employment. I passed the civil service examination for typist and was assigned to serve in U.S. Veterans' Hospital 63, Lake City, Florida.

There, a new door of service for the Lord opened to me on Sundays and after work hours. First, I began by showing my Africa pictures in churches, and then with stereopticon projector and Bible slides, I began to give lectures in country churches and schoolhouses. On Sundays, I took Ruth and the children in our car and went to some of these country places to help in the Sunday School, and then I preached in the meeting afterwards. I soon had preaching places twice every Sunday and stereopticon Bible pictures nearly every night in the week. I paid the expenses for oil, gas, and tires for our car and received no money for my services.

Two or three miles east of Lake City was a little sawmill town called Watertown with an abandoned Baptist church. Ruth and I went out in the car on Saturday afternoons when I didn't have to work and visited from house to house and re-opened the church. We soon had a nice Sunday School going with preaching services afterwards and also stereopticon Bible lectures at night. However, it was not long before an old Baptist preacher, Rev. Eubanks, came along and said it was his church. We willingly stepped down and let him run the meetings. We still helped with the Sunday School. He held a communion service, but we were not invited to partake of it because we were not regular members of the Baptist church. I told my children they were not Christians just because we were missionaries and had taught them the Bible, but that they should be converted just like anybody else.

At a series of revival meetings in that church Bob, Roy and Bessie went forward and confessed their faith in the Lord Jesus. Soon afterwards brother Eubanks immersed them in a little creek nearby. Ruth had been sprinkled as a girl in the Presbyterian church but now was not satisfied with it. She went along with the children, and brother Eubanks baptized her too. He wanted me to go in also, but since I had already been immersed by an Independent Baptist preacher, I refused. Dr. Torrey once told me, "It is not the person who baptizes that makes the baptism valid, but the faith and obedience of the one baptized."

I had annual leave of thirty days with pay from my work in the hospital. We spent the thirty days driving in our car up to a Christian life conference led by Dr. Robert McQuilkin at Greenville, North Carolina. We received much blessing and enjoyed the conference greatly.

Grings Family in SC - 1929

During our trip, we had slept in a tourist camp where there were swarms of mosquitoes. We were always careful to sleep under nets in Africa, but here in the United States of America, we didn't think there was any danger. A short while after we got back to Lake City our little son Grant Fuller came down sick with the fever. I gave him a dose of quinine and thought he would get better.

One of the hospital doctors passed by our house the next morning after I had gone to work and stopped in to see our sick child. He came and told me, "Mr. Grings, you have a very sick child with Tercerian malaria. You had better get him to the hospital." I telephoned the city hospital, and they sent an ambulance and took him to the receiving ward, but it was too late. All the injections and treatment they could give him were of no avail. He died that afternoon, and the next day we laid our dear little Grant to rest in the Lake City cemetery.

With the loss of Grant, I sought a change and secured a Civil Service appointment with the Prohibition Border Patrol in Tampa, Florida. Of course, the patrol officers had to be strictly temperate as far as drinking was concerned, but they had no hesitation in sitting around in my office talking about their intercourse with lewd women. One officer boasted how he had taken a girl out of Sunday School and seduced her. I rebuked them and threatened to report their filthy conversation to the Chief Customs Inspector. That was too much for them, and they had me discharged.

We stayed on in Tampa through the winter, attending various churches and helping in a Baptist mission among Spanish-speaking people who worked in the big cigar factories. I talked by long distance telephone with the business manager of the Veterans' Hospital in Lake City, and he agreed to reinstate me in my former position. I moved all our household stuff back to Lake City with our car and trailer. We settled back into our former way of living and preaching the gospel.

FATHER'S FAMILY TREE

My father Hilar Grings was born January 15, 1862, at Dubuque, Iowa, U.S. America. He died on his little truck farm near Stockton, California, January 20, 1932, of cardiac decompensation due to mitral insufficiency, so said Dr. Lynch. He constantly smoked a pipe, so nicotine was the cause of it. He was buried in Park View Cemetery, nine miles south of Stockton on Manteca road.

Here is the family tree: GRANDPARENTS: Peter Grings, 1820-1884, and Barbara Landin, 1834-1923. UNCLES and AUNT: Leo, 1873-1950. Adam, 1871-1933. Barbara, 1868-1948; her husband, B. J. Scherr, 1866-1941; their children: Gertrude, Florence, (Dubuque, Iowa), Ralph and his wife Helen and two children, Louisville, Kentucky. UNCLE: Hugo, 1865-1943; his wife Hannah 1864-1930; their children, Carl, Hazel and Barbara, Waterloo, Iowa. UNCLE: William, 1858-1944; his wife Carrie, 1859-1941; their children, William and Nettie, Des Moines, Iowa.

ENCOUNTER WITH BOOTLEGGERS

My father left me an inheritance of $2,000. My mother came to live with us in Lake City and often went with me to the country meetings. She still had a sweet soprano voice and loved to sing duets with me in the meetings. One night, I took her and all my family in our car and went to a meeting which we were holding in a little country church. We started early so I decided to drive by a bootlegger's house and invite him and his family to the meeting.

It was growing dark and as we turned a corner I could see a light in his house, but suddenly it disappeared. I drove the car up to the gate in front of his house and waited for someone to come out of the house. It was all dark on the porch, and I thought perhaps no one was at home so turned the car to go. Later his wife told me that he had come out on the porch and raised his pistol to fire at the car, thinking it was a police car, but she had pulled his hand down.

As I turned the car to go, "BANG!" went a pistol shot and I heard something hit the side of the car. I swung the car in front of the opposite house where lived the father and mother of this man. The old man opened the door a wee bit in the glare of my headlights and said, "Who's doin' the shootin'?" I said, "It's not me; it's that fellow over there." The old man slammed the door shut. I turned out the lights and stepped on the gas to make my getaway. "BANG! BANG!" went shotguns, and I felt the shot whiz past the window. But, by that time I was far enough away that it did me no harm, and I kept going. When we arrived at the church I let my wife and mother and the children go in, and then I took my flashlight and examined the side of the car. There was a hole where the pistol bullet had passed through and lodged in the spring cushion of the seat in which my mother had been sitting. Two inches higher and it would have entered her back and probably killed her. Another miracle was that my little daughter Louise had been sitting in the seat back of her grandmother with her legs in the path of the bullet. She had moved over just before the man had fired, so was saved from being shot in the leg.

The next day I drove back to the bootlegger's house and showed him the hole in the car. I preached to him and tried to persuade him to turn to the Lord and be saved. But he had been taught that a man was predestinated to be saved *or lost*, and there was nothing he could do about it, so he would make no move to repent and accept the Lord Jesus as his Savior. I could have reported him to the police and had him arrested, but I would let nothing hinder the work of the gospel and kept on with the meetings.

In recording God's marvelous protection of Louise at this time, it is in order that I tell of other instances of protection. One night when Louise stepped out the kitchen door in the dark, she fell head first into a little barrel filled with rainwater below the edge of the porch. Her mother did not hear it but felt the impulse to come out on the porch and saw the little feet sticking out of the rain barrel and snatched her out before she drowned.

Bessie was leaning against the car door while we were driving down through Tennessee. The door jarred open. She fell out, but the door swung shut and held her feet until I could slow down and pull her back in. All she suffered was a little skin scratched off from her fingers from her hand dragging on the ground, and a good scare!

Bob climbed up between the fence and outhouse where we lived and fell and hooked a projecting nail head in the corner of his right eye, tearing the lid. They brought him to me where I was working in the hospital. Dr. Willis sewed the eyelid together, and it healed without any permanent injury to his eye. On the ship coming from Japan, Bob fell down a stairway with a pop bottle in his hand when the ship pitched heavily. The pop bottle broke and almost severed his little finger. We bound it up, and it healed but left it stiff. Otherwise, he suffered no injury from the fall. Also, on the *Mexico Maru*, coming from Mombasa, he rolled off the hatch in his sleep during the night and cut a gash in his forehead but was not seriously injured. Many times the Lord protected the children. Surely children have guardian angels.

On May 6, 1933, at Lake City, Florida, Mark Bowden Grings was born. It was his mother's desire that he be baptized in the Presbyterian church, and I yielded to her wish. We presented him at the morning service and the Rev. Dr. Montgomery sprinkled water on his head in the name of the Father and the Son and the Holy Ghost. Years later in the Congo, on profession of his faith in the Lord Jesus as his Savior, I immersed Mark.

THE *HILTON* DISASTER

In 1933, the depression hit the United States. Banks went broke, and President Roosevelt began laying off government employees in order to economize. They laid me off, a man with a wife and five children to support, instead of the pretty young woman in the same office who had a husband with a drug store. I said to Ruth, "That is just the Lord giving us a push to go back to Africa." Without any mission board backing us or promise of pay from anyone, we set our faces for Africa.

Anton Andersen, who had worked in the Alur tribe near us in the Congo, and Miss Alma Doring of the Unevangelized Tribes Mission helped us with a letter which said we were "antinomiously" associated with that mission. We were thus able to get a passport visa to enter the Congo. My mother had seven or eight thousand dollars in the bank and relatives with whom she could live, which made me feel free to leave her for the gospel's sake. With the $2,000 which my father had left me when he died and what we had saved up, we had nearly $3,000 in hand. A first-class steamship ticket would cost at least $1,500. We sought for a cheaper way to go.

Someone said, "Why don't you go on that old sailing ship at Fernandina seaport?" I had been closing some of my stereopticon lectures on Africa, by showing a beautiful picture of a sailing ship and singing, "If you'll just send me across the deep blue sea, I'll tell them of my Savior and of how he died for me. I'll tell the story to them if you'll just send me." The first verse goes like this, "Far across the deep blue ocean in a dark and dreary land, a million souls in darkness dying fast on every hand. They never heard the story of how the Savior died, nor of the Roman soldier who pierced his side." Apparently the Lord took me at my word that I was willing to go even on a sailing ship.

I went down to Fernandina and found there at the customs dock a big four-masted schooner, the *Augusta G. Hilton* of Boston. She was due to sail in a few days for the Cape Verde Islands, just off the west coast of Africa, which would put us in direct line with steamships going to the Congo. I told the captain we were missionaries and asked if he would grant us passage on the ship. Captain Pereira said he could not take us as passengers, but we could sign on as crew. I readily agreed to do that and asked him how much we would have to pay. He said, "How much will you give?" I made a quick calculation of about half the cost of the steamship ticket and said, "Eight hundred dollars." He took me up immediately, and we signed on as "crew."

Some time later I learned that the old sailing ship had brought a big cargo of salt from the hot, desert Cape Verde Islands where it seldom rains. They had put the salt up on the beach at Fernandina, but a tidal wave or something had washed it away, and they had no money to pay customs and port charges. The ship was put up for auction, but nobody wanted to buy a sailing ship.

A sawmill man named Sahlman calculated that if he could get the ship by paying customs and port charges he would be able to load her up with lumber and telephone poles and send her back to the Cape Verde Islands where they had no wood and thus make his money back. So he bid her in for about $800 - a ship that cost $250,000 to build! It seems I was the one who bought the ship because I paid the $800 in cash.

There was plenty of room in the big holds of the ship, so we were permitted to take all the baggage we wanted to take, free of charge. I still held to the policy of medical work and industrial work as well as schoolwork. We spent about a week buying our outfit: medical supplies, carpenter tools, pit saws, typewriter, mimeograph, printing press, sewing machine, grist mill; fifty-three cases of goods. Then, I put in my car and trailer. To me, the most valuable piece of equipment in my outfit was my stereopticon projector and 1,200 slides of Bible pictures which I intended to use in teaching the natives the whole Bible.

As I was leaving Jacksonville on the last trip to the ship, a little voice whispered in my heart, "You don't have a camera." I hadn't planned to take one. At that moment, I was passing a pawnshop and saw a little Brownie box Kodak in the window marked for sixty-five cents. "Well," I thought to myself, "Sixty-five cents is nothing." So I bought it and three or four rolls of films. (Later, it proved to be the most valuable thing in my outfit and was about the only thing besides clothing that we saved from the sinking ship.)

Grings Family on the *Augusta G. Hilton*

The Reverend J. M. De Vette, pastor of the Baptist church in Fernandina came down to see us off, and we prayed on the beach like Paul and his company did. The Coast Guard tug towed us out of the harbor into the Atlantic Ocean. Then they hoisted the sails, and we were on our way once more to the Congo, the one place of our hearts' longing and desire. Captain Pereira gave up his big comfortable oak-sealed cabin in the poop for Ruth and the girls and baby Mark. Bob, Roy, and I had another cabin. We had included a good big bill of groceries in our outfit from which we could add from the ship's fare such articles as we desired.

The *Hilton* was an American-built ship but manned by Portuguese officers and crew. Captains Pereira and Wanon were of Portuguese blood, but the First Mate Frank Rosario and the eight crewmen were of African descent. One crewman had his wife and baby with him on board. All of them spoke English as well as Portuguese.

A STOP AT BERMUDA ISLANDS

The wind was moderate but the Gulf Stream off the Atlantic coast is always choppy. The ship rolled and pitched considerably, ripping the sails. They lowered them for repairs, which caused hours of delay. The captain set a N by NE course toward the Bermuda Islands in order to catch the trade winds which would waft us across the ocean to the Cape Verde Islands.

After two or three days sailing, the old ship began to leak so badly that they put in to Bermuda Islands. This was surely in God's good plan, for we made friends there among the Portuguese Christians of the Brethren Free church, who afterwards helped to support us in the Belgian Congo. They entertained us lovingly in their homes, and I spoke many times in their meetings.

A diver was sent down and put a lead patch over the leak in the ship's bottom. The owner, Mr. Sahlman, came up from Fernandina and sold part of the cargo of lumber to pay expenses. They embarked thirty-one Portuguese men and women passengers going back to Portugal by way of the Canary Islands. About August 1, we set sail from Bermuda.

THE *HILTON* ABANDONED AND FIRED

Ruth and I and the boys settled down to study the Kikongo-Commercial language. Things went smoothly for about a week. We did not strike the trade winds as expected, and there was not enough wind to fill the sails. The ship began to leak again. The forward fresh water reserve tank had sprung a leak, and all the fresh water had leaked out into the bilges, so there was no fresh water to spare to make steam to work the pump. They tried using salt water in the boiler, but this soon clogged the injection pump. Finally, they turned to the hand pump and bailing out the water with buckets.

My son Roy had made him a little toy sailing ship. He said, "Dad, I think there is enough water down in the hold to sail my ship on if I could get the wind down there."

The crew had not been paid their wages, and they did not want to work. They broke up the hand pump, and then there was no way to pump the water out of the ship. As the water continued to rise in the hold, the poor old ship took a list to starboard. If the cargo of lumber floated and shifted, we were in danger of being capsized. We prayed the Lord to send a ship to our rescue. The captain estimated that we were about eight hundred miles from the nearest land. There was no radio on the ship. I had been showing my stereopticon slides and preaching to passengers and crew twice a week. The last lecture I gave was on Paul's shipwreck. That night I took my projector up on the roof of the after cabin and flashed its bright beam in all directions, but there was no answering signal from another ship.

The next morning the captain ordered all of us to make preparations for abandoning ship. The big steel life boat and the little wooden ship-to-shore boat were lowered into the sea. I persuaded them to make two rafts from hatch covers and lower them into the sea. The Portuguese passengers began putting so much baggage into the big lifeboat that I protested that it would sink. Captain Pereira set the example by throwing his bag overboard. They took no thought of embarking fresh water. I had some difficulty in persuading a man to help me fill two small barrels with water and hoisting them over into the lifeboat.

It was about noon, August 18, 1933, in Lat. 39 N. Long. 41 W. when Captain Pereira gave the order, "Everybody in the lifeboats!" I brought my family on deck, and we tied on our life jackets. I said to Bobby, "Bob, are you afraid to die?" He said, "No Daddy, I'm trusting Jesus." When he was converted those years previously in Lake City, he came home from the meeting and said, "Dad, I used to be afraid to die, but tonight it is all gone." Now here he was actually face to face with death and he could still say, "I'm not afraid to die."

We were assigned to the little ship-to-shore boat with Captain Wanon and six of the crew and a Portuguese young man from Bermuda named John Perry. The boat was so heavily loaded that it was only about twelve inches out of water when we all got into it. Thank the Lord the sea was calm and the sun shining brightly.

The Burning *Hilton*

As soon as we had put off from the ship, Captain Pereira had kerosene poured in all the cabins and set the ship on fire to make a big smoke signal for other ships to come to our rescue. What a sore test of faith it was to sit in the lifeboat and watch all that big outfit of fifty-three cases of goods: automobile and trailer; four bicycles, typewriter, printing press, my precious stereopticon projector and 1,200 slides, all burning up! However, I had an inward peace and confidence that it was all for our good. We still had the omnipotent God for our help and refuge.

ONE STEP FROM DEATH

About 4 p.m. a storm blew up. Clouds came down as black as night. As we prayed, the Lord held back the rain. Not a drop fell on us, but now the sea began to rise in great swells and water splashed into the little boat. Death was not far off. The little wooden boat had no watertight compartments like the big steel lifeboat. It would sink with the first big wave. Just then, a shout went up from the seamen, "STEAMER!"

RESCUED BY THE *HERCULES*

The Dutch freight boat *Hercules*, Captain H. J. C. Zindler commanding, came up rapidly and dropped us a sea ladder. We climbed up onboard and sat down with thanks and praise to God for saving us. Fifteen minutes later the storm broke, and rain and wind whipped the sea into raging white caps. Oh, what a wonderful Savior Jesus is! The Captain of the *Hercules* said that surely it was God who had sent him with his ship to pick us up in that out-of-shipping-lanes part of the Atlantic Ocean.

Grings family in a Lifeboat

His reckoning at the time was Lat. 37-26 N. Long. 40-51 W.

Captain Zindler said the day before, (when we were praying the Lord to send a ship to our rescue), a storm beat so violently on the bow of his ship that he had to change his course. That brought him directly to our sinking ship at just the moment most needed. That night his radio operator sent out a general call for ships to be on the lookout for the burnt hulk of the *Hilton*, but he received no answer to his call. Apparently there was not another ship in all that region. Without God's direct intervention, we would all have been drowned.

One of the officers vacated his room for us. Ruth and the girls slept in the bunk, and the boys and I slept on the floor. Meals were served to us in the crew's mess room before or after the officers and crew ate. The Portuguese passengers and crew were quartered in the between-decks space of one of the large holds of the ship and had their meals there. Altogether, there were forty-three of us, so food had to be limited because the *Hercules* was not provisioned for so great an emergency. I had a religious meeting on deck to give thanks and praise to God for saving us. Captain Zindler and his officers and crew not on duty attended, as did the Portuguese.

PUERTO RICO TO CANARIES

Captain Zindler decided to take us to San Juan, Puerto Rico. In four days, we sighted the high green mountains of that Island. Oh, how good it was to see land again! We had been twenty-nine days out of sight of land. When we entered port and the ship tied up to the dock, the U.S. port officials took no immediate action in disembarking us.

After two or three hours wait, I went ashore and called at the customs office to make inquiry as to what to do. The officer said there was no appropriation of funds to meet our case; he was sending a cablegram to Washington for instructions. I went back to the ship and told Captain Zindler. He said if it were in Holland, they would land and take care of us and make inquiries later. It was clear to me that we, being U.S. citizens on U.S. territory, would have to shift for ourselves.

I took my wife and children ashore with the one bag of clothing we had saved from the *Hilton* and left them sitting on the steps of the government building while I went to search for a place to stay. The Methodist missionaries kindly took Mrs. Grings, Bessie, Louise, and Mark into their home. Mr. Bueno, Secretary of the YMCA, gave Bob, Roy, and me lodging and meals in that institution. The Portuguese Consul eventually placed the Portuguese passengers and crew in a hotel until they could get passage to Portugal.

My wife was rather discouraged with the loss of all the trunks of clothing, dishes and household equipment and wondered if we should return to Florida. I said, "No, that is just the Devil keeping the gospel from Africa. We still have some money, and the Methodist missionaries have given us clothing.

Let's go without any outfit." After praying it over together, she agreed; so I hurried around getting passage and visa. I found a big Spanish passenger ship going to Spain by way of the Canaries and booked passage third class for there.

Grings family on the steps of the Puerto Rican Capitol

When we boarded the ship, there was such a crowd of people on deck that I gathered my family under a lifeboat and waited. I was dreading going down into the third-class compartment with all those "peons." When the ship cast off lines and started out of port, one of the ship's stewards came to me and asked for my passport. He took it and went back to the purser's office. Soon, he came back and beckoned us to come with him. He put us into a nice second-class cabin with six bunks and forced ventilation without extra charge.

In the Canary Islands, we met strong Roman Catholic opposition, but Misses Florence Isaacson and Ausherman of the Pentecostal Mission took us into their home and lovingly entertained us for the week or ten days we were there. When I tried to get passage on a ship for the Belgian Congo, the Roman Catholic shipping agent told me there was no room. Another ship came into port, and I asked for passage on that. The agent objected that my passport was not in order. A third time I tried to get passage on a Belgian ship that was tied up to the dock, but the agent would not receive my U.S. dollars.

CANARIES TO CONGO

Then a ship came by and anchored outside of the harbor. I said to my wife, "We are going on that ship tonight." Soon after dark we took what baggage we had gathered together and went down to the landing. The ship's boat was there just as if it had been sent for us. I asked the boatman if he would take us out to the ship. He readily consented. When we came alongside the gangway, there was no one to stop us, so we took what baggage we had and climbed up on deck.

The purser came out and asked what we wanted. I told him we wanted to go to the Belgian Congo. He asked to see my passport and when he saw that the visa was in order he asked if we had any money. I showed him some $100 bills. The shipping agent who had refused me passage so many times was standing nearby and the purser asked him why he had not given me a ticket. He replied that I did not have the "Pesetas." The purser told him that our U.S. dollars were good and to take me ashore and make out a ticket for us. When I got back to the ship, I found my wife and children happily settled in a big second-class cabin with all the comforts we needed. They also gave us a special table and waiter; so we were as well off as we would have been in first class.

After twelve days with stops at various ports, we disembarked at Point Noire, French Equatorial Africa. Mr. Berg of the Swedish Mission kindly entertained us until we got passage on the railroad that was being constructed to Brazzaville. We went third class to save our money and found it comfortable enough, except that there was no drinking water on the train or at the stations. Everything they drank either came from a liquor bottle or a teapot. The kind missionaries at Brazzaville helped us get on across Stanley Pool to Leopoldville, and we were in the Belgian Congo once more, praise God.

FAMILY MINISTRY IN CONGO AGAIN

Now we began to understand why God permitted all our big outfit to be sunk in the ocean. He wanted us to move lightly and rapidly. With all that big outfit we never could have gone back into the dense jungles very far from the river. We would have had to settle down on the riverbank and tried to bring the natives to us. God wanted us to go to the natives. Therefore He permitted the material things to be taken away from us so we would trust in spiritual things. However, we did buy some second-hand household goods that had been left at Leopoldville by missionaries going on furlough. From Leopoldville, we went by river steamer to Kikwit and then by company truck around to Idiofa, and finally by bicycle and porters and carrying chair through a rainstorm to Tshene, the mission station of our old friends the Anton Andersens.

We were eager to go on and find an unevangelized tribe in which we could open a mission station. After a week or ten days of delightful fellowship with the Andersens, he helped us raise a caravan of porters and we started out. We passed through the small Balore tribe, but I did not find a suitable place for a station among them. Finally, we came down to the Kasai River below Mangai, and I went over in a canoe and made contact with some men of the large Bankutu tribe.

CHRISTMAS AMONG THE BANKUTUS

The men wore raffia palm fiber loin cloths, painted their bodies and had leopard and crocodile teeth and other fetishes about their necks much like the Balendu people among whom we had worked for eight years in east Congo. They understood the Lingala language which I had learned at Aru and Aba. I explained to them who I was and what we wanted to do in their tribe. They readily agreed to come and carry us back into the forest to their village.

I went back and told Ruth what I had found, and she was

enthusiastic to enter this tribe. We crossed the crocodile-infested Kasai with all our baggage and equipment in three tippy canoes and found the Bankutu men waiting for us. We had three bicycles. Ruth took little Mark on her bicycle, and I took Bessie and Louise on my bicycle. Bob and Roy rode their one bicycle in relays. The porters followed, and so we started back into the jungles.

We camped in the first village. The government rest house had only one room; and when we put up our camp cots amidst all our baggage, there was no room to move around. The next morning was Christmas 1933. The children sat up in bed and opened what presents we had to give them while the naked boys and girls and men and women looked in at the open front of the rest house. I told them the Christmas story and preached to them in Lingala. The headman interpreted.

OSHWE TO LOKOLAMA

We stayed there about a week, and my children made friends with the Bankutu children and Ruth with the women. Then I took my bicycle and went a day's ride through the forest to the government post at Oshwe on the Lukenie River. The officials were surprised to see a missionary come out of the forest from that direction. They marveled that we had entered their territory by that seldom-traveled route.

One of the officials spoke English perfectly. I explained to him that we wanted to open a mission station in a part of the tribe where the people were entirely out of touch with civilization or a Roman Catholic mission. He told me the Bankutu tribe had an estimated population of 32,000 people. He was the Agent Territorial over the Lokolama territory in the northeast part of the tribe. He said that two or three of the villages were very wild and had not yet submitted to the government, and it would be dangerous for me to enter in with my family. Moreover, it would be very difficult to bring in European food, and we would have to live almost entirely on the native food. I told him we had already served ten years among the savage tribes of northeast Congo and could live on the native food.

The officials were dubious of my proposition to enter that territory, and they said I would have to take the risk of hunger and hostility. I assured them that we were fully aware of the danger and difficulty of living among these savages, but God had just recently brought us through shipwreck in the ocean, and we were sure He would enable us to establish a mission station in this Bolongo clan of the Bankutu. The Administrateur Territorial sent police to call porters for us, and I went and brought my family out to a large village near the government post Oshwe, where we remained for a few days until the Agent Territorial returned to his post at Lokolama. All the while we were studying the language. My children learned it as rapidly as I did.

It had cost quite a bit of money to pay those caravans of porters and to move about. Our funds were low, but those dear friends we had met in Bermuda sent us liberal gifts which enabled us always to pay our expenses without asking anyone but God for help. Our greatest difficulty was in getting checks cashed. Traders and government officials helped us in this. About the middle of January 1934, we started for the Bolongo clan of the Bankutu tribe. It was a ten-day portage from Oshwe to Lokolama.

We passed through many big villages where the people had never before seen a white woman and white children. Sometimes the native women called Bessie and Louise *bekaji* (spirits or ghosts) and pulled their long hair or pinched them to see if they were really flesh and blood. The girls quickly learned enough of the language to talk to the women and girls and not only tell them who they were but also who Jesus is. The official left one of his black soldiers in a certain village, not so much to protect us as to keep the people from running away for fear of us, the *bekaji*, as they called us. The official entertained us kindly at his post at Lokolama for a few days and called the chiefs and headmen to talk with me. They were friendly and favorable to our living among them.

MBONGO STATION

We moved out to a village east of the government post at

Lokolama and began looking for a station site. Early one morning I took my bicycle and rode on to the east through forest and plain, passing through four villages, until I came to the village of Mbongo. There I met an intelligent headman named Kankai. The Belgian government had carried him out of his village as a young man and trained him to be a soldier in World War I. He spoke three languages, Kingwana, Lingala, and his own language Lonkutu. Here was a man who could not only interpret for me, but he was also acquainted with the outside world and the white man's ways. He said there were two more villages to the east and a path led north from Mbongo to the big chief Zulumpembe's village Munja. Very plainly this was the center of the Bolongo clan. I went back and brought my family to live in the little government rest house while I built our first temporary house of poles, thatch and bark.

There was a small plain here called Itsiku with a large grove of trees in the midst of it. My wife and I decided this would be an ideal place to escape the heat of the tropical sun. I hired the village men to make a clearing in the midst of it just big enough for our house. They brought building material; and by the first of March 1934, we moved into our mission house. The official came to visit us and agreed that we had chosen a very good site.

But all was not smooth going. While we were still living in the rest house, I became sick with some kind of stomach trouble and could eat nothing but a little gruel or soup. The native people had been bringing us many bananas and ripe plantains. The rest of the family ate of them freely, but I could not eat even one without vomiting. I kept on working on the house as much as I could without food until my legs wasted away to "pipe stems," and I had to lie down on my bed. A native man visited me and said he knew a man who had recently died of that same trouble. It made me angry, and I determined I was not going to die and went ahead building.

The next morning a Roman Catholic catechist from a distant village appeared at the door with a large bunch of spinach greens to sell to us. The Roman Catholic priest had introduced the seed into the village. The catechist had planted it but didn't want it for himself. When he heard of this new white family at Mbongo village, he made the two-day trip to bring the spinach greens to me. I paid him a good price; and when Ruth cooked some of the greens for me, I could eat them without any nausea or bad effect. After two or three meals of this tender spinach, my stomach trouble cleared up, and I could eat again as usual. Apparently the Lord used this Roman Catholic catechist to bring me just the remedy that would cure my stomach trouble.

I had been afraid to come away back here ten days into the jungle without any European food, but now we found that there was plenty of wild antelope and pig meat which we could buy from the natives very cheaply. We learned to like their *kwanga* bread, made from the fermented and steam-cooked roots of the cassava plant. Pineapples, bananas and plantains were abundant. In the adjoining Bolendo clan, they had rice to sell. In place of sugar, we bought large gourds full of wild honey from them.

The one thing that was hard to bring in from a distance was salt. We could use salt in trading for eggs and chickens. With the food and housing problem solved, I began leaving my wife to run the station and school while I went on preaching trips to the villages for a week or so at a time. One or more of the children always went with me. They helped greatly by telling Bible stories to the native children. Years afterwards when I baptized some of the converts, I asked them when they believed in Jesus. They said, "It was when Bessie and Louise told us about Jesus raising Jairus' daughter from the dead."

Two young lads, Bosangi and Bashomia came at irregular intervals from Lomasa village east of us. They wanted to learn to read. No matter if it was just at noon when we were sitting down to eat, my wife would leave the table and go out and teach them. They also went with me on preaching trips. Two other boys in Lompole village, Mvula and Botu, learned to read; so it was necessary that I make a translation of at least the gospel of Mark.

We prayed for a language helper; and one morning a fine upright man, Bosesa-nkoi, dressed in short pants and shirt and wearing a tropical sun helmet, came to our door. He said he wanted to work for me. On inquiring into his history, I found that he too, like Kankoi, had been drafted into the Belgian Army and sent as a soldier in World War I, to British East Africa. He spoke three languages and had attended meetings of missionaries. He could read and write and was employed as secretary to Chief Zulumpembe, but now he said he wanted to work for a man who had a heart like his heart.

Bosesa-nkoi became my faithful language helper, and we translated the Gospel of Mark, songs and Scripture verses into Lonkutu. He also traveled with us on preaching trips. Too bad I never baptized him. He eventually went back to his distant village for a while and died of amoebic dysentery. Bosangi afterwards took his place when I translated the book of John.

One morning, Bessie ran into the house and said there was a white man coming up our path. I went out to meet him and was overjoyed to find that it was Mr. Angus Brower, one of the unmarried missionaries we had met at Tshene. He stayed with us a few days. Then I took him over to Dekese Territory, and he opened a mission station at Bosanza village in the Isoldu clan. After about a year, he went back to Tshene and married Anton Andersen's daughter, Emma.

THE LEOPARD

Once only did I see a leopard in the jungles, but no doubt they often saw me. One time I was riding my bicycle rapidly down a hill to a little stream in the forest and surprised a big leopard that was lying on a tree which was bent down just above the water. He was fishing. He held his face down close to the water, and if a curious fish should come up to have a look at him, he would snatch it out in a flash with the sharp claws of his paw.

When he saw me he made a leap for the opposite bank but fell short a little and splashed into the water. He scrambled out with an angry growl at getting wet and disappeared into the jungle. Usually the wild animals will not attack you if you do not attack them.

Another time I stopped at a little stream to drink and wash my hands and face. Then I went on, pushing my bicycle up the steep hill. There had been a heavy rain the night before which washed the path smooth and I saw no tracks on the ground. When I came to the top of the hill, I remembered that I had left my glasses by the water. I turned around and started down the hill to get them. There, in the middle of the path were the fresh tracks of a big leopard! He had been following me uphill; but when I turned to get my glasses, he sprang away into the forest, and I did not see him.

RUTH'S DEATH FROM BLACKWATER FEVER

Mr. Brower was the only white person besides the government official who ever visited us at Mbongo. Mrs. Grings did not see a white woman for over two years, until she made a four-week preaching trip with Roy down to Oshwe and all the way to the Swedish Baptist Mission in the Basakata tribe.

When she came back, she became very ill with the blackwater fever. The nearest doctor, if there was one, was at Oshwe. It would require twenty days for a messenger to go and the Doctor to come to us, so I did not send for him. We sat by her bedside and watched and prayed, and for a time she seemed to be recovering. She even got out of bed and went to the village to help a woman in childbirth. This overtaxed her weakened condition, and she went back to bed and lost consciousness. I couldn't get her to swallow even a spoonful of water. Like a candle burning lower and lower, her life burnt out.

June 21, 1936 after the morning service and our noon meal, the girls were relieving me at Ruth's bedside while I was taking a little rest. Bessie came and called me saying that Mama had ceased to breathe. My wife and the mother of my children was gone! Oh, what sorrow filled our hearts!

During the afternoon we chose a grassy place at the edge of our grove of trees and dug the grave. The next morning two of the village men came and carried the body on a cot down to the little chapel I had built in the village. All the people gathered for the funeral service. They had never seen such a funeral before. Truly we wept tears, but we made no loud shouting and wailing like they did over their dead. We sang hymns, and I talked to them about the happy home in glory where Mama's spirit had gone. I promised them that they too could go to that beautiful village of God if they would put their trust in the blood of Jesus Christ to save them.

They asked to look upon the dead. I uncovered her face, and those semi-naked men and women, boys and girls, passed by in a line and looked with wonder and respect upon the cold, calm white face of the one who had often told them about Jesus and taught some of them to read. Two of the men carried her body to the grave. For lack of a better coffin, I placed it in a hollowed-out log with a slab for a covering. Thus with hymns and prayers, we buried her in that faraway jungle grave. We wept not as those who have no hope. The funeral service was a testimony to the natives which changed many of their lives. In the years that followed, her grave was a silent testimony for Jesus.

Ruth Grings' Grave Marker

But she left a more enduring monument in the form of two beautiful royal palms at the village of Mimia. These palms grow only down by the Lokoro River. She had brought some seed back with her from a preaching trip down there and had planted them in the village of Mimia. When I passed there a year or two later, our teacher Loyona pointed to these two beautiful flourishing palms and said, "Those are Mama's palms. She told us about Jesus."

Some time before her death with the help of the village men, I had made sun-dried bricks and built us a new and permanent house, but she was permitted to enjoy it only a few months before her death.

THE PIGMIES

The Administrateur Territorial called me to Oshwe with witnesses to report the death of my wife. I left Bob, Roy, and Mark with Bosesa-nkoi to keep the house and teach the school and took Bessie and Louise with me for that twenty-one-day trip to Oshwe and back. Bessie had learned to ride her own bicycle, but I carried Louise on my bicycle. As previously, on our entrance into the tribe, the girls were the main attraction. We had crowds of people to preach to in every village. In one large pigmy village attached to a Bankutu village, the little people became so excited that a headman shouted in my ear, "Run, or they will kill you."

The path was clear and smooth going out of the village, so we jumped on our bicycles and soon left the threatening mob behind. A year or so later, Roy and I also had a narrow escape from one of those pigmy villages. They were the only ones who ever threatened us with violence. But the gospel brought a change among them, and when missionary Oscar Anderson visited them in 1942 or 1943, some of them asked to be baptized.

It was a trying experience for Bob, Roy and Mark to be left alone for those three weeks, but it prepared them to form another gospel team. They had learned to preach the gospel really well in the Lonkutu language. After talking and praying it over with them, Bob and Roy volunteered to take their bicycles and cooking pot and go out to preach the gospel in distant villages. They stayed out about ten days; when they returned, they said, "Dad, we could have stayed out longer if we had taken more salt with us." It was easier to buy food with salt than with Congo money.

About that time, five of the young men whom Ruth had taught to read, Bosangi, Bashomia, Mvula, Bola, and Botu, asked to be baptized. My little daughter Louise also wanted to be baptized. After due examination and instruction, we went to a nearby forest stream, and the little white girl led the black boys down into the water for me to baptize her and them. We returned to the village chapel and observed the Lord's Supper, using a cup of sweet pineapple juice in place of wine, and native *kwanga* in place of wheat bread. The Spirit of God came down and blessed us with unity and love for one another just as well as if we had been in a beautiful temple with real wine and individual cups.

LIVING IN THE VILLAGES

With these young men to do the teaching, we opened regular schools in their villages. I visited their schools occasionally to help. However, my services were limited to a day's trip because I could not leave the children alone. We talked and prayed the matter over and decided to close the station and take some of our things which were really necessary, and go out and just travel from village to village without returning. This we did and reached nearly all of the sixty villages of the Bankutu tribe once a year.

In one of the villages, the son of the witchdoctor was converted and wanted to be baptized. His father had made him keeper of the fetish or idol which they called *Ikopo*. We told the young man that he would have to publicly burn the *Ikopo* before we would baptize him. He said he was willing to do so. But when he went into the house to bring it out, there was a great cry from his father and other elders standing around, "Don't burn the *Ikopo*! You will die! You will die! All of us will die if you burn the *Ikopo*."

The young man drew back in fear of their cry. Again we told him that he must burn the *Ikopo* and trust the Lord Jesus to protect him from all the power of the devil. The young man took courage. He put some sticks and firebrands together and blew on them till they blazed up. Then he ran into the house and brought out the *Ikopo*.

Very few people ever get to see the *Ikopo*. This one was the skin of a little animal something like a bear. It was filled with roots of bushes supposed to have medical power, bones of certain animals, pieces of white clay, human hair, a tooth, and I don't know what else. He brought it to me and said, "You burn it." I told him it was his fetish, and he must burn it.

The father and others were still crying, "Don't burn the *Ikopo*! Don't burn the *Ikopo*!" Satan was pulling the young man that way with the group of heathen, and the Lord Jesus was pulling him this way with our Christian group. The Lord Jesus won. With a mighty effort, the young man threw the *Ikopo* into the blazing fire while we all joined hands and circled around it singing, "*Bolo ne jin-ande-e-e; Bolo ne jin-ande-e-e. Balungu ba Yesu atoika. Bolo ne jin-ande.*" (Glory to His name; glory to His name; the blood of Jesus will save you. Glory to His name.) The young man was so full of joy that he leaned over backward with his shoulders in the smoke to show that he was not afraid of even the smoke of the burning *Ikopo*. I baptized him, and he became a leader in the village church.

We had many encounters with these witchdoctors. During a meeting in one village, the witchdoctor interrupted me and asked, "Why should a man go to hell if he never had heard of Jesus?" I hesitated to answer. Bessie spoke up for me and said, "You don't go to hell because you never heard of Jesus. It is because of all the wicked things you do." She went on to name some of the things witchdoctors do. That stopped his mouth, and he went away.

Roy was preaching at our meeting in another village and telling the story of Abraham and Lot. The government official had been in that village a short while before. When he left, his big pussycat stayed behind. She was having a hard time living among the dogs in that village. When we arrived in the rest house, pussy immediately came and made friends with us. At the meeting, she was sitting on a log with Bessie and Louise. When Roy came to the part in the story where Abraham's servants and Lot's servants were having a quarrel, two yellow dogs ran into the meeting place and began to fight. Pussy raised her fur and got set to fight. Roy kept on preaching and told how Abraham said, "Let there be no strife between us for we are brethren." Just then the pussy leaped from the log and slapped those dogs right and left with her sharp claws and chased them away. The people looked on with wonderment to see this living example to Roy's preaching. We always referred to this cat as "Pussy the Peacemaker."

As Bessie grew strong and gained expertise in riding her bicycle, she began to carry Louise in front of her. I bought a little black chick for them as a pet, and they carried it in a little basket on the bicycle. When we arrived at a rest house, they would put the little chick down and hunt roaches and termites for it to eat. It followed them wherever they went. They named it "Ebony."

One day we were preaching in a village, and Bessie was telling the story of the Rich Man and Lazarus. She told how Lazarus died and was carried by the angels into Abraham's bosom where he was content and happy. Ebony was scratching in the dust in front of her, and he turned over on his back with his feet up in the air and twittered in perfect contentment.

The natives looked on with interest. Bessie went on with her story. She told how the rich man died, and in hell he lifted up his eyes and said, "Father Abraham, send Lazarus to dip his finger in water and cool my tongue, for *I am in torment in this flame*." She said that in such a terrifying voice that Ebony jumped up and ran behind her. The natives laughed, but Ebony's action helped to drive home the truth that hell is a place to greatly fear.

Another story is about "Mia," the little monkey whom they had for a while; when he died, they had a funeral for him. Also, "To-Whitt" the little owl died from the indigestible fiber of palm nuts which we fed him. They also had a funeral for him and for a beautiful pigeon who got caught in a trap set for crows. Altogether they had quite a cemetery.

THE TOPOKA-TOPE STATION

In the year 1937, we came out of the Boldi clan near the government post at Bena-Bendi on the Kasai River. We found a beautiful grove of trees, Topoka-Tope (groves-two), on a rolling hilltop in an extensive grassy plain. After successfully preaching the gospel in the three surrounding villages, we decided to make a station there. It was a much more beautiful site than that of Mbongo, with a broad view across the valley far away to the hills along the Kasai River.

There was another large government post with shops and mail communications at Basongo, just across the river from Bena-Bendi. We could go in on our bicycles one day, get the mail and provisions and return to Topoka-Tope late the next day. Then too, it was only two days travel on to Port Francqui, at the head of the Cape-to-Cairo Railroad; and yet there were hundreds of people in this territory who had never heard the gospel.

One day, I took Louise with me on my bicycle and went to Basongo. We received our mail and came back the next day. About noon, we were passing through the big plain above Bena-Bendi. It was the dry season. Hunters had set fire at the edge of the plain to drive out the antelope where they could shoot them with their bows and arrows. There was no wind, and the fire was burning lazily along. I sensed no danger and rode on into the midst of the plain with Louise walking behind the bicycle. Suddenly a wind sprang up; (Satan is the Prince of the Power of the Air), and the flames came leaping towards us. Smoke closed in, obscuring the view. I stepped on the pedal to make speed and get ahead of the fire. The chain jammed, and I had to jump off and push the bicycle.

The fire was rapidly coming nearer. I left the path and tried to push the bicycle through the long grass. The fire leaped over the narrow path and came racing towards us. The smoke was so dense I could not see which way to go. Just then a little voice whispered in my heart, "This way! This way!" (Isaiah 30:21) I followed the Spirit's guidance and immediately came to a patch of *green* grass. We ran into it and the fire swept by on both sides. When it was past and the smoke cleared away, we looked this way and that, over the blackened plain, but there was no other spot of green grass in sight. I looked at Louise's dress: not a spark had fallen on it. Then we remembered Isaiah 43:2, "When thou walkest through the fire, thou shalt not be burned; neither shall the flame kindle upon thee."

THE PYTHON

Another interesting thing happened at Topoka-Tope: I was opening a path down into the ravine to our water spring. Two native men were following me to clear the path with their bush knives. As I neared the spring in the dense jungle, I heard something go, "Swish-swish." I went a little further and heard it again. I stepped up a little elevation where I could see down to the spring, and there lay a great python coiled up. She had swallowed an antelope, and her middle was so swollen and heavy she could not crawl away. Her head and a couple feet of her body were raised up above the swollen belly, ready to strike out in defense.

I called the men, and they came with their bush knives but were afraid to approach the great python. I became impatient at their delay and took one of their bush knives, cutting a long pole and sharpening it at the end. Then I approached the python and as she struck out with her mouth wide open to grab me and draw me into her coils, I jabbed the pole into her mouth and pinned her head to the ground till one of the men came up and hacked it off.

The python was over twelve feet long and so heavy that they had to tie a pole to her and carry her up to the plain. We opened her belly and pulled out the dead antelope which had horns six inches long and weighed about forty pounds. She also had twenty or more eggs in her belly.

I gave them a good sermon from that dead python. I said, "You see she came to her death because she swallowed up the antelope and could not crawl away. That is the way it is with Satan. He swallowed up the Lord Jesus on the cross, and now he cannot escape. He is a defeated enemy. This antelope is dead, and we took it out of the snake's belly, but the Lord Jesus is alive. He rose from the dead, and now death has no more power over a believer."

SEPARATION FROM BESSIE AND LOUISE

But all the while, missionary friends were advising me to put the girls and Mark in a school or some place where there were white women to care for them. At Port Francqui, I bought an old Fiat car, and we started out bag and baggage for the American Presbyterian Congo Mission School for white children at Lubondai.

But the car broke down, and we landed at the APCM mission Bulape. Missionary Washburn thought they could make a trailer out of the old Fiat and took it in payment for carrying me and the children two days in his big truck around to Mr. and Mrs. Haller's station at Mangungu, in the Bambundu tribe.

They agreed to receive Bessie and Louise and take care of them for what I could pay. Bob, Roy, Mark and I went back to the Bankutus. However, we were not happy without the girls. After three and a half months, I went to Mangungu and brought them home to Topoka-Tope.

We never stayed long at Topoka-Tope. After about a year of itinerating through the Boldi clan, we made the long trip back to the Bolongo, always preaching two or three times in each village we passed through. The missionaries Mr. and Mrs. Visser and my old BIOLA schoolmate Miss Mary Kolachny invited us to their station at Booke among another tribe. We carried all our necessary clothing, mosquito nets and blankets on our bicycles and went to that station. Bessie and Louise wanted to stay there, and so I left them and little Mark with the Vissers to teach them in school with their children. Bob, Roy and I went back to our village work in Bankutu land.

ENCOUNTER WITH AN ELEPHANT

Some time later we were riding through the forest for two days on our bicycles from Oshwe to the Kasai River. At night we slept in the forest with a fire on each side of us. We heard elephants in the night, but they smelled our fire and passed on. We started out the next morning without further thought of them. As I was riding down into a ravine ahead of the boys, suddenly I heard a great scream like a steamboat whistle. I clamped on my brakes and stopped. There at the side of the road in the underbrush was a mother elephant with her baby by her side. She looked at me and I at her. I wanted to turn and run back, which probably would have been fatal in causing her to chase me. But the verse in Genesis 9:2 came into my mind, "The fear of you and the dread of you shall be upon every beast of the earth."

I said in my heart, "Lady elephant, I know you are afraid of me; and if you don't do me any harm, I won't do you any harm." Then I walked and pushed my bicycle by her, and she let me pass. I turned and motioned to Roy to follow. She let him pass. Then the baby elephant ran off into the forest, and the mother followed it. The great beast could easily have trampled us to death, but the Lord held her back.

BAPTIZING THE CONVERTS

We had made many converts in the Bolongo and Bolendo villages. Some of these converts in the village of Mimia said to me, "Tata Mandefu, (my native name meaning 'Father Beard'), why don't you baptize us? The Roman Catholics say we are not Christians because we have not been baptized." I said, "Good! Everybody who wants to be baptized, come with me to the river." About half of the village followed me to the river.

I was not expecting so many, but with the help of Bob and Roy to examine the younger ones while I examined the men and women one by one, we found about twenty people in that village who gave clear testimony to their salvation through faith in the blood of the Lord Jesus. I baptized them, gave them the Lord's Supper and formed them into a local church, with the unanimous approval of the group that Loyona and wife should be their spiritual leaders and teachers. After that, in nearly every village they asked for baptism. During the year, I baptized over five hundred converts and organized them into local congregations with a teacher or leader who was married and could read.

Among the five hundred or more people whom I baptized, there were no more than two or three old men. If a person is not saved when he is young, it is not likely he will be when he gets old. The older one becomes, the harder it is to break off sinful habits and receive the Lord Jesus. One old man whom I baptized was a convert of his slave. In times past they had war with another tribe, and he had captured this boy and made him his slave. Now as a young man, the slave was converted in our meetings, and his life was so changed that the old man was converted by his testimony. He said to his slave, "You used to be lazy and disobedient. You would steal and lie to me and do many bad things. Now you work and do what I tell you, and you don't steal and tell me lies. How is it?"

The young man told him it was because he had given his heart to the Lord Jesus, and He had washed it and made it clean in His blood. The old man accepted the Lord Jesus as his Savior, and he too was made pure and clean through the blood. When I put my arm around him to baptize him, I felt that I was holding a precious jewel in God's kingdom.

Another young man whom I finally baptized was at first held up because he could not confess Jesus as the Son of God. From the beginning of those baptisms I had been led to make this question the first and decisive one, "Who is Jesus Christ?" When I asked this young man, "Who is Jesus Christ?" he became nervous and made an evasive answer, "Oh, He is the great teacher." I said, "Botu, if you don't know Jesus, I will not baptize you. Wait till the next time." I baptized the other converts and gave them the Lord's Supper.

Then I went to this young man and asked him, "Botu, why couldn't you tell me who Jesus is?" In an agony of spirit he said, "Oh, Teacher, it was because I had an elephant fetish hidden in my house." He had said that he had put away all heathen customs and fetishes. But, like Ananias and Sapphira, he had lied to the Holy Ghost, and the Spirit would not let him confess Jesus as the Son of God. "No man can say that Jesus is the Lord, but by the Holy Ghost" (I Cor. 12:3). Later Botu brought out his fetish and burnt it and made the good confession, and I baptized him.

TRANSITIONS AND VARIOUS TRAVELS

The Swedish Baptist Mission (SBM) sent a young man missionary, Mr. Bodine, to work in the tribe, and I loaned Roy to work with him for a while and help him learn the language. Mr. Bodine did not hold to the strict requirements of separation from sin and heathenism that we taught. However, he did persuade the people to build schoolhouses and chapels in many villages and greatly developed the schoolwork.

Grings and O. Anderson Families - 1938

We eventually left the Bolongo and Bolendo clans, and the SBM took over. The SGM (Scripture Gift Mission) had printed one thousand copies of my translation of the Gospel of Mark, and the BFBS (British and Foreign Bible Society) had printed a like number of my translation of the Gospel of John into Lonkutu. Therefore, the believers who had learned to read had the printed Scriptures and typewritten copies of our hymns in their own language. However, the SBM pushed these to the back and did all their teaching in the Lingala trade language, in accordance with the decision of the CPC (Council Protestant du Congo) at Leopoldville.

While we were attending a missionary conference at Kikwit, word reached me that the Vissers had taken Mark to the Methodist missionaries at Wembo-Nyama. I made the long trip over there on my bicycle and brought him back with me. I had been hoping to have the girls also back with me again. At Topoka-Tope, we had planted some beautiful tiger lilies in the shade along the path leading to the plain. They all turned their lovely blossoms towards the sunlight that was reflected from the plain. My heart was looking that way too in hopes that Bessie and Louise would return. The next day a storm of wind and rain came up and beat the lilies to the ground. That was the way it was with my hopes and longings for Bessie and Louise to return. The missionaries had won them away from me, and they never came back. First it was my wife taken from me by the blackwater fever, and now it was my daughters.

December of 1942 we attended a conference of the UTM (Unevangelized Tribes Mission) missionaries, and they requested me to take over the mission station at Iwungu in the Bambunda tribe while missionary Kroeker was on furlough. Bessie, Louise and Mark went to the Kajiji station where they were in the Mennonite Brethren school for a year. Bob went to Cape Town, South Africa to attend the AEB (Africa Evangelistic Band) Glenvar Bible School. Only Roy remained with me. We went back to the Bankutus and continued our village work for several months; then we too started out on our bicycles for South Africa by way of Booke. Roy, however, decided to go to the APCM (American Presbyterian Congo Mission) mission school at Lubondai where Bessie, Louise and Mark were now located. I went on alone.

A TRIP TO CAPE TOWN AND BACK

I had a glorious ministry preaching and giving missionary talks in churches, schoolhouses and country farms where I stopped the night. I met Bob at the AEB school near Johannesburg, and he went with me for two or three days on his bicycle to visit the Scheepers family near Peris. Then I went on alone. The Salvation Army lady major at Bloemfontein gave me her own bed to sleep in and next took me to their Sunday School picnic and had me speak in their meetings. At one country farm where I stayed the night, the wife and mother of the home was a Protestant believer. She was bewailing the fact that she had sent her daughter to a Roman Catholic school, and now the daughter was making prayers to an image of the Virgin Mary which she kept in her room.

Arriving at Cape Town, I met the "Missionaries' Friend," old Mr. Rowland of Wales Street Baptist Church. He helped me get a place to stay in the Salvation Army hostel, and showed me many other kindnesses. I went out to Mowbray and visited the Davises who had been missionaries under the Africa Inland Mission when I first went to Congo. His wife Laura was a cousin of my wife. I climbed or rode my bicycle part way up Table Mountain and visited the Cecil Rhodes Museum and Zoo. When I revisited the AEB Bible School at Glenvar, the director did not have much time to talk with me and was unwilling that I should take Bob back to the Congo with me, as Bob was now a member of the AEB and committed to work with them in the Congo. Thus, I lost my main helper and companion for our work in the Congo.

LAST DAYS IN THE CONGO

When I got back to the Congo, Roy had been drafted by the American Consul at Leopoldville for World War II. I took my bicycle and started out alone to revisit all of those Bankutu villages again. Oh, what a lonesome and heart-breaking trip it was to come to those familiar places where we used to sit down in the forest and eat our food, have a bath at little streams, or where we stopped to pray before entering a village to preach to the people! Some times there was such a lump in my throat that I couldn't drink water.

At the Christmas holidays, I went to be with the children at Lubondai. Mark and Louise went off with their schoolmates to spend the vacation with them, but Bessie stayed with me. We made a trip to Elizabethville and then with Bishop Springer to his Methodist Episcopalian station and college at Mulunguisi. Bessie and I prayed the old year 1945 out and the new year 1946 in. We asked the Lord if it was His will for us to return to the U.S. that He would send us the money to pay the passage, which would be about $3,000 for the four of us. Years before, my mother had deposited money in the Pacific States Saving and Loan Bank in California, jointly in her name and mine. She died in 1937. The bank went broke, and I thought that was the end of it. When I came back to Topoka-Tope, I received a letter from my legal representative, Oscar Zimmerman of the Immanuel Mission to Seamen, Berkeley, California, saying that the bank still had $3,000 for me if I would waive the interest and use the money to buy a *steamship ticket* to return to the U.S.! The reason for the last provision was that during war times, money could not be sent out of the U.S. except for bringing U.S. citizens home. In that remarkable way, the Lord kept the exact sum of money we needed shut up in that defunct bank until we were ready to return to America. If we had received the money when my mother died, we probably would have spent it or lost it in some other way like I lost the inheritance from my father with that *Hilton* shipwreck. All praise to our blessed Lord Jesus.

Bob was returning to the Congo to work under the AEB on their mission station. I wrote him to get permission to come with me for a month or so to make a final visit to our Bankutu villages. Likewise I wrote to Bessie to cut her schoolwork short at Lubondai and come with Bob when he passed on the train. Louise and Mark decided to stay and finish their school year, but Bob and Bessie sent word for me to meet them at Port Francqui.

BITTEN BY AN ADDER

When we left our house at Topoka-Tope, we couldn't lock it up to prevent stealing, so we dug a cellar in the bedroom and put our trunks and household stuff in it. Then we laid logs over the top and covered it smoothly with clay, so no one would know there was a cellar there. I opened up this cellar to let it air out. The next evening I picked up a trunk and stepped down into the cellar with my bare feet because there was loose sand in the hole. As I did so I felt something sting my heel. I jumped out and looked at my heel. There were two drops of blood about half an inch apart. I took a light and looked into the cellar. There was a small but poisonous adder which had bitten me in the heel. I killed it with a bush knife and put it in a tin can on the table so if I died, the people would know what it was that killed me.

The poison burned like fire in my heel, and soon I began to vomit. Then I felt my heart flutter and thought my end had come. I knelt down and told the Lord that I was not afraid to die because I knew He had saved me. It seemed heaven opened, and I could see the beautiful city. I wanted to go, but a little voice whispered, "What will become of your children who are expecting you to meet them at the railroad station?" I said, "Yes, Lord, for my children's sake, heal me of this snakebite." It seemed a pressure came on my right side, and I vomited blood. Then I was sure I would not die. I pulled the table up near the window and laid down on it where anybody who passed by could see me. I sang hymns and resisted the devil all night.

The next morning my heel was still burning like fire, but I resolved to go to meet the children in spite of it. I loaded my bicycle and started out, riding and pedaling with one foot when the path was level, but hopping along and pushing the bicycle when it was uphill. It took me about two hours to get to our first village. The natives helped me get on to the Kasai River where I found a canoe waiting. I passed over to the motor road on the other side and finally got to Port Francqui. The poison went up my right side, and there was a lump the size of a large bean about to enter the back of my head. A doctor gave me an injection of antivenom which stopped the poison, but my foot was numb for a long while afterwards.

THE RETURN TO AMERICA

My children came in on the train and rejoiced at my salvation from the snakebite. The three of us went on our bicycles through the Boldi, Bolendo, Bolongo, and Isoldu clans, preaching, baptizing, giving the Lord's Supper, and bidding farewell to our beloved Bankutu people. When we arrived at the AEB station Kondji, Bob bid us goodbye and rode away on his bicycle to join John Scheepers with whom he was to work under the AEB, and I haven't see him since, (now November 4, 1963). Thus ended my thirteen years of constant service to the Bankutu people.

Bessie and Herbert

Bessie and I turned our bicycles and headed for America. We passed through Dekese and Baluba land and then wearily followed the motor road up hill and down through Badinga and Bambunda land to Mangungu, where we joined Louise and Mark. Angus Brower took us in his car to Kikwit where we obtained passage on riverboats to Leopoldville. I had some difficulty in getting the $3,000 from the bank, receiving only a small part of it in U.S. dollars. I asked the immigration officer for a return visa to Congo, but he put me off saying that I could get it in Belgium. This was at the close of World War II, and many people were seeking to return to Europe. One had to have priority to get passage on a ship. We passed over to Brazzaville, French Equatorial Africa. The Swedish missionaries there, as in 1933 when we arrived in Africa, kindly entertained us and helped us get passage on the train to Pointe Noire.

A big U.S. Army transport, the *Ernie Pyle*, had been assigned to carry passengers, but there was no room for us. We had to wait till it made the trip to Belgium and returned. An old Portuguese trader who spoke English was kind to us and rented us two rooms where we lived and cooked our food very cheaply during the wait. An American "Liberty ship" came into port, and I tried to get passage on it, but they were not permitted to carry passengers. However, the officers and crew were very kind to us and invited us on board for a sumptuous supper. I preached to them and visited the ship several times. The steward said to me after the evening meeting, "I have been a member of the Methodist church for many years, but I had to come to Africa to learn the way of salvation."

Practically no one spoke English in Pointe Noire. I was glad to hear of an English woman, Mrs. Lewis, who was living in the hotel. I went to see her in her apartment. She had two children, a brown boy and a black girl. She said, "That is one of my mistakes." She had a long story to tell of being deserted by her husband, and having no way to make a living she was "peddling her virtue" for money. We invited her to take supper with us a time or two. Bessie even gave the woman her own Bible. We tried to be kind and helpful to her, but apparently it was in vain for she continued to receive the city judge in order to pay her hotel bill, if indeed she paid it. I was able to get into the city prison a time or two and preach to the prisoners. We attended services in the Swedish church and were entertained in their homes. The British Vice Consul also entertained us once.

At last, the big transport *Ernie Pyle* returned, and we got passage on it. The girls were put in a fourth floor below sea level with two hundred or more women and children. Mark and I were in one for the men with triple-deck bunks. I seldom saw the children on the voyage to Belgium. They had other missionary children whom they knew for companions so were happy and content. Meals were served cafeteria style in the long dining hall which occupied the full width of the ship. Everybody had to line up, get their trays and pass by the food counters to be served, and then find a place at some table to sit down and eat. There was an abundance of food.

When we arrived at Antwerp, Belgium, rain was falling, and I delayed till the last in getting ashore. Finally I put on an old raincoat someone had left and went out and searched the waterfront till I found the Leger des Heils (Salvation Army). The kind secretary gave us a big room in which we could stay and eat our meals.

Roy was in the U.S. Occupation Army at Bad Nauheim, near Frankfurt, Germany. We sent word to him, and he obtained a leave of absence and came to be with us for a few days. Oh, how glad we were, and how proud to see him in his new soldier's uniform! I went with him once to the U.S. soldiers' barracks in Antwerp and ate with them and testified to them.

A FRIEND IN THE POLICE DEPARTMENT

I had a hard time getting passage on a ship for the U.S. One day while I was out in town looking for passage, a U.S. Liberty ship tied up to the quay near the place where we were staying. Bessie and Louise saw the American flag waving at the stern and went out unaccompanied to walk on the quay and look at it and other ships. Police in plain clothes mistook them for "adventurous" young girls and carried them off to the police station.

When Police Inspector Rene Pauwels learned that they were the daughters of missionaries to the Congo, he said, "Now you are Protestants, and we are Roman Catholics; please tell me the difference between Protestants and Roman Catholics." Bessie did it so thoroughly that Mr. Pauwels was convinced of the truth. Many of the policemen had gathered to listen to the discussion and Mr. Pauwels told me afterwards that if Bessie kept on preaching she would have converted the police. She ended up by saying, "We'll bring you a Bible and prove it to you."

The next day, we took Bibles and Testaments and went to the police station and preached to the police. Some of them bought New Testaments or a Bible. When we left, Police Inspector Pauwels said to me, "Mr. Grings, we examine many women in this big city, but we have never seen girls like yours." He took my hand in a hearty grip and said, "If you ever need any help, let me know." It was in that remarkable manner that God gave me the friendship of this influential police inspector for an emergency which was to come about a year afterwards.

I visited the U.S. ship which Bessie and Louise had seen and asked for passage. The captain sent me to the office of the ship's agent in the city. The young lady in the office, Miss Doubledeer, was interested in our case but said some Roman Catholic sisters had applied for passage and there was no room for us. I went back to the American captain and told him how I had served in the U.S.

Navy four years and was now bringing my motherless children back to the U.S. for their education. The captain brought his fist down on the table with a bang and said, "I am the captain of this ship, and if anybody goes as passengers, you and your children do!"

But even with the captain's approval, it was hard to get around all those war regulations and Roman Catholic influences. Miss Doubledeer used her influence in the office. After I'd made many visits back and forth to the office, one day she called for me to bring the money and gave me our tickets. When she did so I said, "Do you want to go to heaven?" She said, "Yes, I do." I said, "Here is your ticket," and handed her a slip of paper on which I had typewritten the words, "Cast your burden upon the Lord, and he will sustain you." Not only did *we* get passage on the ship, but other missionaries did too - Mr. and Mrs. Mozer, a single lady and one of Bessie and Louise's schoolmates from Lubondai. We had happy times together crossing the Atlantic.

The ship landed at Baltimore, Maryland. There was a strike on, and the docks were picketed. Mozer and party took a taxi and went out through the picket lines. I waited and got our baggage out on the dock. Along came a laundry van driven by a Jewish boy. When I explained to him who we were, he said, "Get into the van." It was October 16, 1946, and we were back in the United States of America. We crowded in with our baggage, and he shut the door and took us out without any interference. He left us at the Salvation Army headquarters where a lady officer took care of Bessie and Louise. Mark and I stayed in the Men's Hostel. I tried in vain to get the Westervelt Home for missionary children to take my children into their school, but they were not prepared to do so upon such short notice.

I didn't want to spend more money waiting there in Baltimore, so we boarded a Greyhound bus and went to Garrettsville, Ohio. There I finally left Mark with my deceased wife's sister Alice Chapman, and Louise with a cousin's family. Bessie stayed with me, and we went on across the U.S. to Los Angeles. The Church of the Open Door (BIOLA church) took no interest in getting a place for Bessie or placing her in the Bible Institute. I tried Mabel Culter's school for PK and MK (preachers' kids and missionaries' kids). She would not sign an agreement to be responsible for the moral and spiritual care of Bessie. We were out on the street without a home. I telephoned my old BIOLA mate, Marion Reynolds, president of his Fundamental Bible Institute. He said, "Bring Bessie up here to 205 N. Union Avenue; we'll take care of her."

Bessie and Louise

With Bessie nicely placed, I was free to travel all over southern California, visiting old friends and giving missionary lectures in churches and private homes. One home was that of the American Sunday School Union missionary Joe Jenkins and family. He arranged many meetings for me. Eventually he resigned from the ASSU and became a missionary to South America under the New Tribes Mission.

A NEW START FOR THE CONGO

Funds began coming in, and I decided to return to Congo. In Belgium, they had told me to wait and get my return visa to the Belgian Congo from the Belgian Embassy in Washington, D.C. When I applied at that office they said, "You are going to California, just wait and get your visa in San Francisco." Now I applied to the Belgian Vice Consul in San Francisco, and he readily gave me a visa to enter the Congo. I started east, receiving gifts of money from brother Tanner in Theodore, Alabama and brother Todd and brother Grube in Mobile Gospel Tabernacle.

In Florida, our old friends and Pastor Rhodes of Watertown Baptist Church helped me along. At Tampa, I gave my missionary lecture in the big Palma Ceia Presbyterian Church which was only a wooden tabernacle under Pastor F. W. Haverkamp when we lived there in 1932. Now they had a high and beautiful stone edifice with up-to-date furnishings. I thought, "Surely that church will give me a liberal offering to help me return to Congo." But, when the meeting was over, the fine, polished, modernistic pastor just shook hands and politely bid me goodnight, without giving me anything.

When I arrived at Jacksonville, Pastor Thompson of the Baptist church told me by telephone that he had a registered letter for me. When I went to his home and opened the letter, I found it contained a check for $100 which my stepbrother Elmer Kipp sent as, "Wages due me for the time I worked in the office of his Chevrolet-Buick garage in 1928." Then I went to Fernandina and saw Mr. Sahlman. He gave me $500 as a refund on my loss of passage and outfit with the shipwreck of the old four-masted schooner *Hilton*, August 18, 1933. With this $500, I had over $1,000 in hand to take me back to Congo.

After some difficulty, I was able to book passage on a "Liberty ship" sailing from New Orleans for Germany and Belgium. I went to New Orleans to board the ship. When I checked my passport with the Belgian Consul at that port, he said it was okay for entering Congo. I embarked for Africa for the third time.

The ship went first to Bremerhaven, Germany. There I saw some of the wrecks and the devastation of World War II. The ship discharged a large cargo of "war-relief" supplies, which the American army was distributing. Dockworkers, office workers and school children all seemed to be receiving the same emergency rations. On the shipbuilding slips nearby were the remains of submarines which were being constructed under a camouflaged roof of celluloid leaves when the British or American bombers located them and bombed them.

When we arrived at Antwerp, I stayed with members of the Belgian Gospel Mission Church and began to gather an outfit of bicycles, printing press, typewriter, etc., to take to the Congo with me. I checked my passport with the immigration officer, and he said my visa for entrance to the Congo was valid. I needed a priority permit to get passage on a ship. I applied to the office of the Colonial Minister for it. There were two vacancies, one for a Roman Catholic priest and one for a Protestant missionary.

With the recommendation of the Secretary of the CPC, Mr. Coxill, I got in ahead of the two Roman Catholic nuns who had applied for both places and secured my passage. All well and good so far, except that I had to pay some unjust excess baggage charges on bicycles and printing press. Miss Doubledeer in the company office helped me to get this sum refunded later on.

TURNED BACK FROM ENTERING THE CONGO

But, when the ship arrived at Boma, the entrance port of the Congo, the immigration officer Mr. Langhoor, who had been the Agent Territorial at Lokolama when we were there, came aboard and took me off the ship bag and baggage, saying I was not permitted to enter the Congo. Why? They gave no reason. I had signed and sealed affidavits from two of the government officials who had known us and our work for a long time, saying that my conduct and morals were good and that there was no charge against me. My re-entrance visa was given by the Belgian Consul in San Francisco, passed by the Belgian Consul in New Orleans, and approved in the office of the Colonial Minister in Antwerp.

They put me in the CMA (Christian and Missionary Alliance) home, promising to pay my board, which they never did. The missionaries tried to get some action on my case, but nothing was done. They wanted me to pay my passage on a ship back to the U.S., but I refused saying I had returned with valid passport and visa and already had paid out nearly a thousand dollars for outfit and passage. I wrote a letter to the governor of the Congo, but no reply, silent contempt. Finally, the American Consul at Leopoldville wrote me a brief letter saying, "You are an undesirable person."

I stayed there three months hoping and praying that a way would open for me to go back to the Bankutu people. Once they did give me a false hope by asking if I would put a deposit of fifteen thousand francs. I promised to do so. They asked me to show the money to them. I lacked part of the ready cash, but one of the CMA missionaries at Boma, gentle Miss Jean Robson, bought both of my bicycles, and I took the money and showed it to the officials. When they counted it, they backed out, as it was only a "bluff," thinking I would not have the money, and they could use that as a reason for keeping me out of the Congo.

Besides preaching in soldier barracks and in individual homes outside of the town, one good thing I accomplished during my stay at Boma was to read the life and works of George Müller, which stayed me up with faith. One old missionary of the CMA urged me to join up with some missionary society under the CPC, and thus I would secure re-entrance to the Congo. But, I wouldn't compromise the faith by joining with that mixed modernistic organization.

After three months, the ship on which I had come to the Congo arrived again in port, and the Administrator ordered me to go aboard. They had compelled the steamship company to give me passage back to Antwerp. When I knew I was to return to Antwerp, I sent an airmail letter to my friend the Police Inspector Rene Pauwels.

SERVING THE LORD IN ANTWERP

The Belgian Gospel Mission gave me a little room with a skylight on the top floor of the mission building where I stayed all that winter while I was appealing my case to the Colonial Minister. Mr. Pauwels went with me in person and laid my case before his honor, the Colonial Minister. I had to make many trips back and forth to Brussels to answer questions at one of the offices. Mr. Pauwels secured the help of the mayor of Antwerp to intercede for me. The American Vice Consul Miss Brying did all she could, but the Roman Catholic authorities were in power and the intercession of these influential people was in vain.

God opened up a large door of service for me in putting gospel literature and Scripture portions on board the many ships which entered the port of Antwerp. I visited an average of three ships a day, five days out of the week, giving the gospel to officers and crews of more than a thousand ships of twenty-one nationalities in about six months. The cleanest ships were Swedish and Norwegian. The dirtiest were Greek. The hardest to obtain permission to board were Belgian, Russian and Spanish. Dutch and English ships would receive my literature kindly, but American seamen would often throw the tracts out of the port or tear them up. Great quantities of gospel literature had been stored with the Brethren church in Antwerp by my old friend and BIOLA mate Oscar Zimmermann of Immanuel Mission to Seamen, Berkeley, California. That was how it was possible for me to have all the literature I could use for this work.

The cold winter dragged by. I had not lived in cold weather since doing Sunday School missionary work in the mountains of Mendocino County, California in 1917; therefore, I suffered from the cold in Antwerp. Mr. Pauwels often had me out to his home for supper. Through my gospel talks with them, he and his wife, and later his daughter Nadia and her lover, knelt down with me and accepted the Lord Jesus as their Savior. I was also welcomed into the homes of the Kruits and Lannens. I spent much time reading at the British Seamen's Mission and the Flying Angel.

OVER IN NORWAY

In February 1948, I went to the Norwegian Seamen's Mission in Antwerp and met a seaman who knew missionary Jense Glittenberg and family who lived at Mangungu with the Hallers when Bessie and Louise were there. This seaman said that Brother Glittenberg lived at Mosterham, near Bergen. I wrote and told him how I had been put out of the Congo. He immediately wrote back and invited me over to Norway.

It seemed useless to try any longer to get back to the Congo; (Satan is wearing out the saints). About the middle of March, I took passage on a Norwegian boat and went to Bergen where Brother Glittenberg met me and began taking me to homes and churches to tell about my missionary work in the Congo; he interpreted. I spent a happy week in his home in Mosterham with him, his wife and five sweet little daughters. I also spoke in the meetings at a nearby church. Besides money, a lady gave me a fine suit of clothes left by her deceased husband. The suit I had worn for six months in Antwerp was about worn out. The gift of this new suit saved me the expense of buying a new one, so I could send more money to Bessie.

All my children except Bob were now at Fundamental Bible Institute at Los Angeles. Roy had been sent to the U.S. from Germany and discharged from the army with the GI bonus which enabled him to pay expenses at Bible institute. Louise and Mark had left the relatives in Ohio and come to be with Bessie at Bible institute, while they attended high school. They sent me a group picture of the four of them. They had so grown in grace and stature that I could hardly believe they were my children.

Grings Quartet: Louise, Roy, Mark, and Bessie

Brother Glittenberg had known Bessie as a little girl of twelve years. When he looked at this picture, he caught his breath and said, "She looks like a queen!" That is what a good Bible institute can do for most any young man or woman who gives him or herself wholly to study and obey the teachings of the Bible.

Brother Glittenberg committed me into the hands of leaders of the Brethren Church, and they passed me on from Haggershund to Christianssand and Drammen, Oslo and Moss. In each of these cities, I spoke many times in their church meetings and homes. They also entertained me in their homes and gave me a bed in the front parlor, which was an honor indeed. Their parlors are beautifully furnished with art vases and oil paintings of Norwegian landscapes so natural that it is difficult to tell if one is looking at a picture or out of the window at the real things.

At Oslo, I visited Mr. Christensen and Miss Hariette Johansen whom I had known as missionaries in the Belgian Congo. Miss Johansen arranged a meeting for me with the King's Guards and interpreted for me. She also operated the reflectoscope when I showed my Africa pictures at other meetings. The newspapers printed some of my missionary articles, one of them illustrated with a picture of Bessie teaching African children.

HOLLAND AND BACK TO AMERICA

In August 1948, I went to Amsterdam, Holland to attend the first conference of the ICCC (International Council of Christian Churches) led by Dr. McIntyre. At the advice of brother Marion Reynolds, President of Fundamental Bible Institute in Los Angeles, I tried to get some of those big church leaders to help me get back into Congo, but this was out of the scope of their purpose at this time. Dr. McCarrel gave me two dollars!

One happy thing I did accomplish, however, was to go to Bussum, Holland, Gueybergstraat and visit Captain Zindler who was now retired. He had brought his ship *Hercules* to our rescue when we were shipwrecked on the *Hilton*, August 18, 1933. He showed me the chart where he had plotted his course for the West Indies but had to change it because of the strong wind and tempest that beat on the bow of his ship that day we were praying for a ship to come to our rescue. He and his wife took me to their church with them on Sunday.

Some time after the ICCC conference, I got passage on a ship and returned to the U.S. At New York I telephoned to the American Bible Society to whom I had given $4,000, money which I had inherited from my mother. They did not invite me to come and see them or attend any church meeting, so I attended the Jerry McAulley Rescue Mission where the famous Christian lawyer Bennett was preaching that night. After the meeting I told him how I had been put out of the Congo, but he could give me no legal advice other than to go to the Secretary of State in Washington, D.C., which I had already planned to do.

I boarded a night Greyhound bus and went on without spending even one night in New York City. I had a stopover in Baltimore and forgot my overcoat when I left on the next bus but recovered it by making a long-distance telephone call back to the bus station. When I found the official in charge of African Affairs in the State Department at Washington, he gave me a long and confidential interview. He said he had all the papers in my case and understood the situation fully. I pleaded that we had fought World War II for four freedoms, one of which was the freedom to worship God according to the dictates of one's own conscience. Therefore the Roman Catholics had no right to shut me out of the Congo. He said that was so, but we have to interpret the law according to the times in which we live. The Roman Catholics have the balance of power in Congo, and we can't oppose them. He said all he could do was to get me a tourist visa to visit the Congo again. Since there was no higher government authority to whom I could appeal, I gave up all hopes of re-entering the Congo and went back to California.

After a sweet visit with the children at FBI, I went out giving my missionary talks and Bible lectures wherever I could find an open door. Always there were gifts of money enough to pay my expenses and some left over to send to Mr. Reynolds for the children.

In late 1948, I boarded a Greyhound bus going to Santa Maria. I had for a seatmate a man from Mexico who had come to California to earn money by picking fruit. I showed him my Africa pictures and he said, "We have some Indians like that down in Mexico, who live near my orange orchard there in Sonora County." He said his house was vacant, and I could live in it while I went to visit the Yaquis. And that is how I got started on a new missionary career preaching the gospel to primitive tribes of Indians in Mexico and South America.

EPILOGUE

The Autobiography of Herbert E. Grings closes at the point where Herbert accepted the fact that his service for the Lord in the Belgian Congo was discontinued, and he was waiting on God for an open door to further ministry. It was 1948: he was fifty-six years of age, a tried veteran of many years and hardships, and *not* a quitter.

For now, we won't go into the details of the ensuing nineteen years spent in Mexico and Central and South America. Many of his experiences there are recorded in his fascinating second book, *Victrola Victories* (1948-1957); others are recorded in his journals which are archived in Northland International University's Global Archives in Dunbar, Wisconsin.

Herbert with a Gospel Recording

Congo doesn't get out of one's veins, however, and Herbert longed to go back. By 1967, he felt his itinerant work among the remote South American Indian peoples was completed. Others would follow and build on his foundation. He wrote in a prayer letter:

> Shall I go back to the Congo and lay down my bones beside the grave of my wife who is buried there? At seventy-four years of age, this is the question that now confronts me. Two of the Congo evangelists and my son Mark who is still carrying on his missionary work there have invited me to return. [...]
>
> These Congo evangelists write, "Teacher, we want you to come and see the seed you have planted in times past." It has not died; the birds have not eaten it; it has grown up and prospered. "Come and see it." My son Mark writes that I could come and put the capstone to the work; and then, if it pleased the Lord, I could lay down my bones besides the grave my wife who is buried there.

And that is what he decided to do. He visited his daughter, Louise Champlin, and her family who were now in Suriname, South America. There they shared the good news that under the new independent government of Congo he would have no trouble getting back in. He was quick to act on the information. The national immigration officer filling in his entrance form wanted to know what a white-haired little old man with no mission board, station, or money wanted to do in the Congo? His simple reply, "My wife is buried here, and I would like to be buried beside her" stirred the astounded official's heart to stamp a permanent visa in his passport, a miracle indeed.

God gave him ten more years of joyful "bicycle evangelism." People were amazed he could still speak the Lingala language and even those first-learned languages from eastern Congo where he began back in 1917. Age and distance didn't stop him. He went everywhere with the same message and fervor on those old jungle trails. He spent time with his oldest son, Bob and family, who were carrying on the gospel work and seeing it expand. Later, he wanted to visit Bessie and Mark (who were now located in South Africa) one more time, but became ill with pneumonia while in the capital city, Kinshasa. With the Father's tender oversight, both Bob and Roy were there. God also arranged another special attendant. In his sick room, Pambo, the son of one of the first five believers back in 1936 at the time of his wife's death, was there to join in the farewell singing of hymns and reading Scripture. What could have been more fitting as Herbert Grings, almost 85, transcended his robe of flesh to his eternal abode! It was November 5, 1977 - sixty years of undeterred service from which he never turned back.

One might ask, "What material possessions did he leave?" He left his hammock that he carried wherever he went, a well-worn Bible, a bicycle-repair kit, and a single change of clothes in a little zippered gym bag. He didn't need anything more! Oh! yes, there was also his passport. Extension pages had been added when he was in South America as he went from one country to another on whatever length of visa he was granted. It opened out like an accordion. A little pang was felt when it was received back from the American embassy with the word "cancelled" in large red printed letters. Well, he didn't need that anymore either. There was no way his body could be transported back the thousand miles interior to where his wife was buried in 1936, but was it not very appropriate for him to be laid to rest in the premier city of Congo?

He did leave his children something of far greater worth than fleeting earthly possessions - a legacy they can cherish and in which they can invest their lives to great advantage, a godly example to follow and seek to live for their generation. When he attained his seventieth year, the age when the priests were to retire from their temple service, he thought perhaps the Lord would take him home, and he wrote his children his final blessing. It reads like Jacob to his sons and Moses to the tribes. What a spiritual treasure he bestowed! His last Christmas, he hand-printed each of his children this message, "My gift to you is a promise to pray for you daily." He couldn't have given anything of more value. We reiterate the words of Psalm 61:5, "Thou hast given me the heritage of them that fear Thy name," and how grateful we are!

Herbert Grings

We will conclude with an appendix summarizing how Herbert's life work has lived on in his children and grandchildren to the fourth generation. Only when we stand before the Lord and it is reward time will we know the full extent of what this one life accomplished for the glory of God and the furtherance of the gospel. May we not be found wanting in our "occupying" till that day!

APPENDIX: Herbert and Ruth's Children

The Autobiography of Herbert E. Grings would be incomplete if the ongoing chapters of this "Adventure with God" were not added. As Abraham of old "went out not knowing whither he went," Herbert Grings did not know what lay in the path before him when he resigned his commission with the US Navy, went to Bible school and on to Africa. Abraham went with promises of blessings that would be worldwide. The life of Herbert Grings could also be said to have spread blessings around the world. We of the following generations marvel at the faithfulness of El Shaddai to direct his path, provide seemingly out of nowhere, protect in dangerous situations and prolong his life past the "threescore and ten" years of Psalm 90:10. God's word to Isaiah in 59:10 is not a suggestion, but a clear command. "My words which I have put in thy mouth, shall not depart out of thy mouth, nor out of the mouth of thy seed, nor out of the mouth of thy seed's seed." We five children were well aware that we had received a "heritage" from God for which we were responsible, and by the good hand of our God upon us, we responded to that heritage. The purpose of this appendix is to give a summary of how Christ's "ye shall be witnesses unto me" commission was carried out. We are deeply grateful to God for this privilege of being His ambassadors to "the uttermost parts." The summary will begin with the eldest, and we will pick up each life where it left off in the *Autobiography*.

Robert Ernest Grings

Winnie and Bob Grings with children

Being the oldest, Bob was the first to leave the family circle and village ministry, to go to South Africa for his Bible training, and then return to the Congo. It should be mentioned here that Bible training was one of the things Dad taught his children was essential, and we purposed in our hearts that, God providing, we would do it. Bob's return to Congo in 1946 was providentially timed just as the three younger children, accompanied by their father, left for the States to get their Bible training. He worked for a time in Congo, with the Africa Evangelistic Band (AEB) missionaries of the school at which he had taken his Bible training, but he was able to make trips to the area where his family had ministered, thereby maintaining a presence there. After Bob completed his service with the AEB mission, he went back to work full-time with the Bankutu people. Meanwhile, two missionary couples and a single lady from the United States came to work nearby. The blessing God had for Bob was the single lady who had recently come to the Congo - just the wife he needed. Winifred Ferrel was from Jerome, ID, and her folks had long been friends of the Grings. What a fine couple they made! In the following years, God blessed them with three children, Ruth Ann, Rebecca and Daniel.

On furlough in 1954, they joined Baptist Mid-Missions; upon their return, they began working again in the Bandundu province. Congo's independence from Belgium in 1960 was a time of unrest and concern, yet Bob stayed through it. The Simba Rebellion of 1964 was what finally forced the evacuation of many missionaries, including Bob and his family. After thirty years of continuous service by one or more of the Grings, they were all out of the country. Mission stations were looted and burned, and thirty missionaries were martyred before the war was over and things settled down again. Bob and his family were among the first to return.

However, the ecumenical movement had come in, and it was necessary for an independent association of Baptist churches to be established. Getting recognition by the government for the organization took fourteen years, but Bob patiently worked at it till it was granted in 1987. Pastors were trained and churches multiplied. God took Winifred home to heaven in 1993, but Bob continued on. His three children married and returned to join in the work. There were grandchildren too. Indeed, for the last decades of his life, he was called "Grandpa" by all, Congolese and missionaries alike. He was a faithful father in the faith. The association leaders gave him the purple sash of a dignitary and an honorary degree was conferred on him in the United States. Weary and worn out, his call to Glory came shortly after his ninety-first birthday in Kinshasa, thirty-four years after his father. Deeply loved by those to whom he had ministered all his life, like Abel, his witness still "speaks."

Roy Gerald Grings

Roy was drafted into the U.S. Army for World II while in Congo, shortly before VE Day, and served in the Occupation Forces in Germany. When he was discharged in the United States, he went right into Bible School training with the GI Bill helping with expenses. Like Dad back in the old BIOLA days, it was manna from heaven to be in classes at Fundamental Bible Institute (FBI) taking Bible Doctrine, Synthesis, Chapter Summary, Personal Work, and other classes while being busy with Christian Service outreach.

Dorothy and Roy Grings with Denise

The "Grings Quartet" as we became known, enjoyed those rich years in a Christian atmosphere under godly teachers with other committed students. Roy went on to seminary at Los Angeles Baptist Theological Seminary after FBI graduation. He was good at languages, having learned several of Congo's tribal ones and having taught himself French; now he added Greek. With that aid, he began the translation of the Bible into the Lonkutu language which he had learned as a child. He married Dorothy Beard, a fellow student, and God gave them a daughter, Denise.

Dorothy was not long-lived, and with Denise married, Roy felt free to return to the Congo. He did not join a mission board; but trusting God to care for his needs, he went as a sort of "tent maker," like Paul working with his hands. He was a tinker in the full sense of the word - a "repairer." Folks would call on him for everything - bicycles, sewing machines, typewriters - and every call was an opportunity, an open door to be a witness. He had a natural talent for music, having carved out a little wooden mandolin in the early Congo days, stringing it with raffia palm twine. He translated a number of hymns and loved to sing for folks wherever he went. Maybe he was not your "model missionary," but his heart was in the right place. When the higher call came in January of 2006, he went on to the land we are to "possess" from God. He missed his eighty-fifth birthday by a few days and was buried there in Kinshasa, another Congo grave. It seems one can almost hear his sweet tenor voice singing these challenging words:

I walked one day along a country road,
And there a stranger journeyed too;
Bent low beneath the burden of His load,
It was the cross, the cross I knew.

"Take up thy cross and follow Me,"
I hear the blessed Savior call;
How can I make a lesser sacrifice,
When Jesus gave His all?

("Take Up Thy Cross," Alfred Ackley)

Elisabeth Charlotte Grings

John and Bessie Gander

With her Bible school completed, Bessie, as she was called, was the first of the four to return to the Congo, in 1951. Our old family location in the Boldi tribe was now the center of ministry near the village of Nkole Nkema, and she began serving there along with Bob and Winifred. Along with a church, a school had been started for the Congolese children; it attracted those from other villages, and boarding school facilities were also built. Village evangelism went on as well on the old bicycle trails, north in one direction and south in the other. Mark and the Champlins arrived in 1954, and Mark and Bessie soon went to the other station at Yassa. The Isoldu and Iyalima clans were reached from there during the dry season, since bridges would be out and mud-slick roads would be very difficult to navigate during the rainy season. The two men, Mark and Darrell, made the strenuous, two-week trip to those villages while Bessie and Louise stayed at Kondji. From there the two ladies made a quick side trip to Booke, the AEB station where they had stayed with the Vissers back in 1942. God was putting His plan together unbeknownst to them. A single young man, John Gander, was there, and God had brought Bessie right to him!

One has to marvel at the ways of God - higher than ours, as He says. Bessie went to work with John at Booke after their marriage, and they were there until the uprisings of Congo's independence in 1960. A daughter, Elisabeth, was born before they were evacuated to South Africa, where a son, John Mark, was born. John had served in the air force in North Africa during World War II, but he had felt the hand of God upon his life so had taken his Bible training and served in the Congo. Now the family ministered in several churches in South Africa, his home country. Bessie was only satisfied if she was witnessing and telling someone how to know the Lord as his or her Savior. One of her key places was a large supermarket. She had permission from the manager to pass out tracts and speak to clients as well as employees, as long as it did not interfere with business. God used this ministry to change so many hearts that the manager visited her home and told her frankly that her ministry had substantially cut down on theft in the store. That is assuredly the power of God unto salvation! Another of Bessie's joyful services was giving to missions. Every penny she could spare was gladly given to the furtherance of the gospel.

But age was showing as she celebrated her eighty-fifth birthday in August 2010, and a month later she bid her loved ones on earth goodbye and joined the ones who had gone before to the Celestial City. Bessie finished her course still in the race, leaving us grateful for the testimony she passed on.

Louise May Grings

Louise and Darrell Champlin

Louise began her Bible school training with the prayer that if the Lord had a life companion for her, he would be there. On several occasions, her father had said, "The most important thing in marriage is to be Scripturally agreed." So how better could this be achieved than by being in the same classes and being taught the same Bible truths? Well, he was there, and it seemed natural being drawn together. Thus, when he suggested that they would make a "good team" for Congo, she readily agreed. This eager young man, Darrell Champlin, was from Salt Lake City, Utah. His mother's spiritual father and mentor had been F. G. Huling, a former BIOLA classmate of Herbert Grings. Darrell and Louise were married after graduation, but they stayed on for postgraduate work. Their first son, David Darrell, was born there.

"Congo or Bust" was sort of the banner as they started out in February 1954. Mark Grings was also ready, so they were a trio, plus little David, headed for New York. Meetings along the way helped pay expenses. Mark would give the slide presentation of the Grings' 1933 sailing, the sinking of the *Hilton* and loss of their entire outfit, as well as the subsequent years of village ministry. Soon, they were on a freighter bound for Congo on a sixteen-day trip across the Atlantic Ocean. A thousand-mile trip interior on washed-out dirt roads and with seven ferry crossings brought them to their destination by the end of June. The couples who had been serving there had left, so they were immediately involved. Of course, Darrell had the language to learn, but it did not take him long to be preaching in the small thatch-roofed church building. There was also a school to keep going and always village evangelism. God blessed them with two more children, Jonathan Mark and Deborah Louise.

Six fruitful years ensued of sowing and watering, teaching and sending out trained men to serve in their villages. In 1964, the Simba Revolution broke out, and evacuation was necessary. Hearing that their station had been looted and burned, many had been killed, and survivors were eking out an existence back deep in the inhospitable forest, their quandary back in the States was, "Where next, Lord?" God honored their lifetime commitment to overseas ministry and opened a new field of service in Suriname, South America.

Arriving in Suriname in 1965, they began working with the descendants of Dutch slaves. The nationals didn't really want them there and distrusted their motives. Why would these outsiders want to come live with them? Darrell and Louise would not have survived that first year had they not been sure they were where God wanted them. They had lived with mosquitoes in Congo, but there were myriads of them here that they couldn't screen out of their small house. And their boots sunk in the mud anytime they stepped outside. Jesus said, "*Be my witnesses,*" and the gospel is "the power of God unto salvation." Forty-seven years later, by God's grace, Darrell and Louise are still ministering in Suriname, and God has abundantly blessed with fruit that remains. God also gave them another son, Ethan Russell, and then called all three sons back to serve with the parents in Suriname. A wonderful "bonus" in this was getting to see their grandchildren born and growing up.

Several trips have been made back to the Congo to see how the Lord is prospering there. Truly, their early labors were not in vain in the Lord. Churches have multiplied, and a Bible college is training pastors. Darrell and Louise also had a ministry as part-time missions representatives for Independent Faith Mission traveling across the United States for about thirty years, challenging young people and churches to "lift up their eyes, and look to the fields..."

In these later years of their lives, their plan is to live out whatever time the Lord has for them in Suriname where there is still so much investing to do. Louise is encouraged by her life verse, "Being confident of this very thing, that He which hath begun a good work in you will perform it until the day of Jesus Christ" (Phil. 1:6).

Mark Bowden Grings

Mark finished his Bible school training in time to accompany the Champlins back to Congo in 1954. They made a good team with an extra driver for the many miles across the States and both men participating in the meetings wherever they were scheduled. Mark presented firsthand the challenge of the field of Congo using the family's 1933-1946 Congo pictures, and Darrell preached Christ's commission to "go." Their visas had not arrived when they made it to New York, delaying them enough to raise some more needed support. In early June, they boarded the freighter *Lindi* sailing from Pier 43 in Brooklyn, NY. It took almost a month to reach the interior station of Nkole Nkema in the heart of Africa, but finally they arrived!

Wyla and Mark Grings

The couple serving at Yassa left, so Mark went to carry on that work. Bessie labored with him until she got married and joined her husband in his work. It was a busy five years for Mark carrying on by himself with church, school, and village trips. As his father had discovered, when one didn't see another white face for months, it got lonely. Darrell and Louise would visit to help personally and in the ministry, sharing with extra preaching and ministry to the women. After a serious bout of appendicitis, it was decided that he should go on furlough to rest and recover. That was when Congo was gaining its independence from Belgium, and he was not allowed to return until December 1960. In 1964, the Simba Revolution necessitated many leaving, but his station was never taken over, so the minute the door opened he was back.

Mark's letters now were really lonely, and a wife was the

answer. But, what young woman would want to live in the jungle situation in which Mark served, doing without so many conveniences? God knew. She was a nurse and midwife with Baptist Mid-Missions who could not get back to her station and was happy to join him. Wyla Weekley was the perfect one to give herself in service with him in this primitive place. Mark later said that he was thankful for the twenty years the Lord had given him there, but the last five were so much more pleasant. A sweet daughter, Esther Joy, blessed their home. Eventually, the ecumenical movement required all mission boards to join or face a fine and imprisonment. So in 1972, Mark's family left Congo and, after a furlough, went to South Africa.

It was slow going at first, but Community Bible Church began in their garage, with King's Kids and other initiatives to reach the neighborhood. A radio program, "Nsango na Bomoi," was begun with Trans World Radio, broadcasting in Lingala back to Congo and neighboring nations. It continues today by transcripts, but the original voice is gone. Thankfully, Robert Marsh, Mark's son-in-law, and the family were there to pick up and carry on when Mark was summoned Home. There were some heart problems, and Mark was hospitalized. Pneumonia set in, and a coma was induced from which he did not awake. In the midst of a busy and fruitful ministry, at age seventy-seven, God took him. His favorite hymn, "On Jordan's Stormy Banks" speaks of the "wistful eye" viewing the "fair and happy land" where his treasure was already laid up. He was "bound for the promised land." It was a particular loss for Louise. They had shared much. Her "little brother" who was only five when their mother was taken, whom she had helped learn to read and had sat with in a darkened room when he suffered with pink eye, was gone. They were the only two who finished high school, had made the voyage back to Congo together, and labored together in the field. Mark had wanted to be sure Wyla was approved and paid Louise's way to his 1968 wedding in Wisconsin. He had received her recent birthday card commenting on the double blessing with the two seven's. The reply from his hospital room via email showed where his heart was: He was so glad the required three months of advance radio programs were completed. His work was indeed finished, and he laid his burdens down to begin his forever in heaven.

This completes for now the telling of the Grings' story, but by the grace of God, it continues around the globe. Herbert and Ruth's descendants are scattered across the world, serving the God of their father and mother. The parents are buried in the Democratic Republic of Congo, and five of their family have already been laid down on the mission fields of the world with them. Three generations of their extended family have returned to the mission fields of the world, and a fourth is being raised there. Of approximately ninety living descendants, over half are missionaries in the uttermost parts of the earth with more preparing to launch out. Many of the remaining family members serve the Lord faithfully in their home countries, whether the United States or South Africa. As a family, these "children" are grateful not just for the godly heritage they have received, but even more significantly for the abundant grace of God which made any portion of this story possible.

Made in the USA
Charleston, SC
19 August 2012